To: Howard and Hunter
From: Donny and Betty
with Christian Love

P.S. This is a book about a remarkable woman of God — Enjoy

"A piece of Florida History"

If you have any questions, corrections or
comments about the book,
please email them to:

dmcbook50@yahoo.com

Second Printing   © December 2012

Dunklin Memorial Camp

The Early History of a Modern "City of Refuge"

…and the Lord commanded Joshua, "Build cities of refuge…"

As told by the Pioneers,
Compiled by Lauralee Evans Bryan

"The Psalm of the Redeemed"

Let the redeemed of the LORD tell their story—
those He redeemed from the hand of the foe,
Some became fools through their rebellious ways
and suffered affliction because of their iniquities.   They
were hungry and thirsty, and their lives ebbed away.
Some sat in darkness, in utter darkness,
prisoners suffering in iron chains,
because they rebelled against God's commands and
despised the plans of the Most High.
They loathed all food and drew near the gates of death
they reeled and staggered like drunkards;
They were at their wits' end.
Then they cried to the LORD in their trouble,
and He delivered them from their distress.
He brought them out of darkness, the utter darkness,
and broke away their chains.
He led them by a straight way
to a city where they could settle.
He sent out his word and healed them;
He rescued them from the grave.
Let them give thanks to the LORD for his unfailing love
and His wonderful deeds for mankind, for He satisfies
the thirsty and fills the hungry with good things.
He turned the desert into pools of water
and the parched ground into flowing springs;
there He brought the hungry to live,
and they founded a city where they could settle.
They sowed fields and planted vineyards
that yielded a fruitful harvest;
He blessed them, and their numbers greatly increased,
and He did not let their herds diminish.
Let the one who is wise heed these things
and ponder the loving deeds of the LORD.

(From Psalm 107 – verses removed and reordered)

"FOR [50] YEARS YOU SUSTAINED THEM IN THE WILDERNESS..."

[ADAPTED NEHEMIAH 9:20]

"Mahanaim"– Camp of God
Genesis 32:1

In Honor Of

My Lord, Jesus Christ.
Friend of Sinners
The Alpha and Omega,
The Beginning and the End of all things.

Dedicated To

My Husband Chris and son, Zeke Elijah Bryan.

In Appreciation for

My Parents - Mickey and Laura Maye
Brothers - Clint, Dean, and David Evans
Grandparents- Earnest and Stella Campbell,
Albert Evans, Edna Walker and Lynn Beville and the other
pioneers who tamed this wilderness and turned it into a
"City of Refuge".

All sacrificed.

"You [did] this because you were looking forward to the joys of heaven – as you have ever since you first heard the truth of the Good News. This same Good News that came to you is going out to all the world. It is changing lives everywhere, just as it changed yours that very first day you heard and understood the truth about God's great kindness to sinners."   *Colossians 1:5,6*

Lauralee Evans Bryan

Many Thanks to Mrs. Nancy Mott, who compiled a large portion of the research for this book.

"The story of Dunklin Memorial Camp is one of the Lord implanting a vision in a person to go out and build a model with the least things to work with except total faith and trust in God, then to expand that ministry by working with the families, and to expand to the third level by training men to become ministers - to continue the work around the world. That's the story that needs to be told."-

Nancy Mott

Juanita & Fred Hibbard

Acknowledgments also to the late "Fred anc Frosty" alumni team of DMC Historians for their archiving efforts in support of this project.

Frosty Bennett

Special thanks as well to:
Chris, Zeke, Mom, Dad, Peggy, and Erin.

"I will thank You Lord with all my heart;
I will tell of the marvelous things
You have done." Psalm 9:1

When a man and his family travel down the 714 "grade" for the first time to enter the program at Dunklin, it can seem as if they are taking the first step on the proverbial "journey of a thousand miles".

The journey of this book has been one of stops and starts...of one step forward and ten steps back. I have been making weak attempts at compiling the stories that make up the history of Dunklin for over 15 years. With the impetus of our 50th Anniversary approaching, I sensed a new urgency to complete the documentation of this incredible story. So I began once more on this journey...

At times, it has felt like a thousand miles to go with no end in sight, and I am so grateful to all those who have encouraged me along the way, and assisted in numerous ways to bring these amazing stories to the light. Though I originally set out to portray the full historical background from conception to present, due to time and space constraints, this edition only covers the very early years and is certainly not the complete picture of where Dunklin has been, or is at today. Instead, it is a distilled representation of the ministry's beginning, and even at that it is difficult to separate out what happened then, from its effect on the current status of things, so the timeline is far from seamless. I do pray the Lord blesses you as we travel together through these pages. I do not profess to be a writer, so I ask upfront that as you read, you forgive any errors, especially those of omission.

The most difficult part about compiling this history has been trying not to leave out any of those who played a key role in making the Camp what it is today. On this point, I am sure I have failed; There have been countless people prompted by the Lord, who sacrificed in so many ways that it would be impossible to mention even a fraction of them.

If you are among these, please accept my apologies and know that your contribution is no less appreciated than those mentioned.

With that said, I want to reiterate here a paragraph from the very first Campfire newsletter printed in 1963:

"We want to sincerely thank all those who have prayed and planned and labored with the Lord; all those who have given of time, materials and money graciously and generously desiring that all the honor and glory go to the Eternal God who commanded Moses to build 'cities of refuge' for those in distress."

Psalm 145

Generation after generation stands in awe of your work;
    each one tells stories of Your mighty acts.

Your marvelous doings are headline news;
I could write a book full of the details
   of Your greatness.

* GOD is all mercy and grace—
    not quick to anger, is rich in love.

GOD is good to one and all;
    everything He does is suffused with grace.

Creation and creatures applaud you God;
 Your holy people bless You.
Letting the world know of Your power for good,
    the lavish splendor of Your kingdom.

Your kingdom is a kingdom eternal;
You never get voted out of office.
God always does what He says,
    and is gracious in everything He does.

God gives a hand to those down on their luck,
    gives a fresh start to those ready to quit.

 Everything God does is right—
    the trademark on all His works is love.

* God's there, listening for all who pray.
    Let everything living bless Him,
    bless His holy name from now to eternity!

              * previous verses omitted

Table of Contents

"The ones who do the planting or the watering aren't important,   He is the One who makes the seed grow… We work together as partners … You are God's [crop] not ours."   I Corinthians 3:7-9

"We can't take any credit for anything you see at Dunklin. The Camp was built by the Lord through the very men who came here for help. Each one has invested a piece of themselves into this ground, literally through their sweat, tears and even a little blood.

Starting Dunklin had nothing to do with us, and everything to do with God. He could have used anybody."

~ Mickey and Laura Maye Evans

Chapter One:
"Shaping the Vessels"

Dunklin Memorial Camp opened its arms to the first of many alcoholics and their families in August of 1962. But the story of how the Camp came about actually began many years before…

Donald Edward Evans came out fighting on January 8, 1932. He got the nickname "Mickey" after his uncle noticed the newborn's tightly balled fists swinging at the air, and compared him to Mickey Walker, a prizefighter at the time. Although he didn't exactly follow in the footsteps of his namesake, he sure did have a fight on his hands growing up as the only child of two alcoholic parents.

His mother Edna was the granddaughter of one of Okeechobee county's original pioneers – Hardee Walker, Sr. A cattleman, he land in Basinger and Okeechobee. He was chosen to travel to Tallahassee to receive the county's founding charter in 1917. She was the eighth and last child of Easter and Hardee Walker, Jr.

Mickey with his mother, Edna

Walker Family

Mickey's father's family had migrated to Okeechobee from Kissimmee. His paternal grandfather, Solon Evans had been a respected chiropractor.

Solon Evans

Mickey as a toddler in Basinger

His father, Albert, was a brilliant man, who loved to read Zane Grey westerns and could recite pages from the poetry of Robert Frost. He passed this love of words down to Mickey, who can remember as a young child hiding underneath the covers with a flashlight and reading late into the night. He l ved vicariously through the cowboy hero's in the western novels. In spite of his drinking, Albert held down a job with Western Union for over twenty years and later kept books for a large dairy farm in Miami.

During the brief interludes that his father would attempt to stay sober, Mickey has memories of him cleaning out the house and hauling away literal truckloads of empty liquor bottles. "He used to hide them everywhere. One day I was playing in the house with a friend. I was mortified when he pulled out a half empty whiskey bottle from my toy box. I had always tried to deny that my daddy had a drinking problem, but it was hard after that. I came to hate the sight and smell of liquor because of the way it affected my parents."

Jerry Walker, Mickey, Tommy Walker
"Cousins in Crime"

Mickey got into his fair share of mischief as a youngster. His uncle had given him a little canary for a pet. The canary met its demise, when the neighborhood cat got "aholt" of it. After finding evidence of the attack, Mickey and his friends arrested the cat, gave it a fair trial, and unanimously agreed to the death sentence – which they promptly carried out.

Another time, Mickey and his cousin Jerry got in big trouble for vandalizing school property when they used their pocket knives to try to escape from the basement of the school where the their kindergarten class was housed by hiding behind a cardboard box during playtime.

He says the little hole they hollowed out in the brick mortar is still there today.

After years of splitting up and getting back together, Mickey's parents finally divorced when he was twelve. Already a drinker for many years, after the divorce, Edna sought to drown her sorrows even deeper in a bottomless bottle.

Often Mickey would be left alone in the house. She would return late in the night after making the rounds of the bars, having to be carried in more often than not, by whatever man she had attracted for the night.

Once, one of her companions nearly ran over Mickey as he hung onto the sides of the truck, begging his mother not to leave. As he got older, he would go searching the bars to find her and get her home to sleep off her stupor. One time he went into every bar in town and pleaded with the owners not to sell his mother any more alcohol.

Mickey began spending more and more time at friend's homes whose mothers would take him in to be sure he got a good meal and safe night's rest. Before he was sixteen, he had moved out of his momma's house and taken up residence in a small trailer Mr. Sam Davis provided for him behind the Twin Oaks Café. Every night, the waitresses would fix up a hot roast pork sandwich up for his supper.

His friends on the "Okeechobee Catfish" football team tried in vain to persuade Mickey to try out for a position on the varsity line up. Mickey had always declined because he knew he had to work to support himself. Finally, and apparently badly in need of players, Bobby Paige succeeded in recruiting him after offering to pay him whatever he was making working at the meat market after school, if he would agree to join up. Mickey's 'paid' football career began and ended with the first practice when he sprained his knee.

Back to his cousin Damon Walker's meat market he went. He worked late into the nights and would frequently fall asleep during classes. His passing grades were a direct result of sitting behind a smart little blond girl whose shoulder he could see over when taking the tests. Most of his teachers knew his situation, and turned a blind eye.

The little blond girl of course was Laura Maye, and shortly after their graduation, Mickey asked her to marry him.

Had she known what lie ahead, she would have likely rejected the proposal.

You see, as a young girl being friends with the preacher's kids, she had vowed never to marry a preacher.

Surely, she must have figured there was no danger of that with Mickey – after all, he had the meat business in his blood. In the two days before their wedding, he and another friend had skinned over 60 head of cattle that had died during a devastating freeze. Exhausted on their honeymoon, he dreamed he was still at it, and began "skinning" Laura Maye in his sleep. That just about earned him an annulment right then and there.

Yet, having experienced God's unconditional love for the first time in his life, Mickey was eager to share it with others. Soon they were holding Bible studies in their little house. Mickey continued working for Damon at the meat market, but work was no longer his "god."

A few weeks shy of celebrating their first anniversary, they were blessed with their firstborn son, Clinton Ira Evans, born January 7, 1952 in the Sebring Hospital.

Clinton Ira Evans, 1952

Mickey was elated to have a "real" family of his own, and determined that his son would never know the pain or poverty of an alcoholic home.

His dream was still to go into the wholesale meat business. He even had a backer. Frank Williamson, Sr. had encouraged Mickey and wanted to loan him the money to start the business. He had the innovative idea of offering folks their choice of live steers right on the premises. It was not to be.

During the year that Clint turned three, Mickey began feeling the Lord's call on his life, which he assumed meant he was to become a preacher. He didn't share this with Laura Maye right away, (maybe she had told him about her vow), but before long, he couldn't hide it from her.

He preached his first sermon at the Brighton Indian Reservation Baptist church to a "crowd" of around 25, half of which were inmates his Uncle Lewis Conrad, the Sherriff, had hauled in to be a "captive audience".
He said it felt like 500. Within ten minutes, he had told them "everything he knew about the Bible" and sat back down so his knees would stop shaking.

Nevertheless, it was the beginning. The beginning down a long road of ministry travelled by small and large steps of obedience that eventually led down the dirt road to founding Dunklin Memorial Camp.

Onnie Jean and Emory Walker

"The first time I heard Mickey preach he was tellin' about the plagues that God sent to Egypt. He told how the Lord said, "I will smite all your territory with frogs." The river would bring forth frogs, which would come into your house, into your bedchamber, on your bed, into your ovens and even into your kneading bowls. Frogs everywhere!

I was sittin' back there listenin' to that, because I was a frog-hunter. I didn't have an airboat and gig. I just swatted them with a cabbage stalk. I was thinkin' to myself if I could have been there, I would have made enough off of those frogs to get rich!"

— Emory Walker,
Mickey's cousin, successful business man, and
Long- time Dunklin Supporter

Emory Walker

Authors Note:
This printing is dedicated to the memory of Emory Walker and the exemplary life of service to his fellow man he lived.

Chapter Two:
Laura Maye's Side of the Story

My mother, Stella Elizabeth Jamison, was born in 1900 on a farm in Boones Mill, Virginia. After graduating from high school, she attended Bridgewater College in Roanoke, VA, Radford State Teachers College, and then on to Bethany Seminary in Illinois.

Stella was preparing to be a missionary to China, but following WWI the communist party was gaining a foothold in China resulting in civil unrest. At the same time, China was being invaded by Japan.

So the door closed there, and Stella changed her plans and accepted a position in Basinger, Florida teaching in a one room schoolhouse.

Mrs. Campbell with her students

After being in Florida for a few years, she married Lamar Campbell. One day while working on the Flying B ranch, both were struck by lightning. Lamar was killed instantly, but Momma was rendered unconscious.

Not knowing how to drive, she walked nine miles to get help.

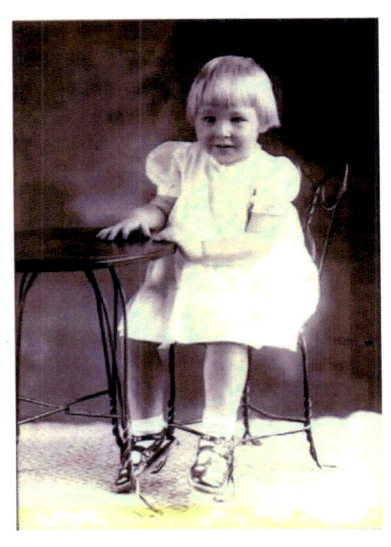

In Biblical fashion, a year later, Lamar's brother Ernest, married his widow. They moved to Okeechobee where Mama taught school for thirty years. My daddy was employed by the Okeechobee Ice Company. During the depression, he gigged frogs on Lake Okeechobee to sell for extra income. He purchased land a little at a time back when an acre sold for one dollar and began raising cattle.

When Mickey and I were seniors in Okeechobee High School, our Civics teacher Mrs. Dee Harvey invited us out to dinner at her and Mr. Basil's place to get us together. That night Mickey picked me up in an old piece of a car he had won the use of in a poker game.

When we got ready to come home, the car wouldn't

start. I thought, "Oh boy. That's it for you, Buddy." We did eventually start dating after that, and by the time we graduated together, we were "sweethearts".

Okeechobee High School Graduates , 1950

Mickey smoked three packs of cigarettes a day and didn't go to church, so my parents weren't too keen on him at first. To appease them, he started coming to church with me. It wasn't long till they loved him as much as they did me, I think.

One time Pastor C.C. Kurtz was preaching a revival meeting, and Mickey accused me of telling the preacher everything about him.

I said, "I didn't talk to the preacher about you!" It was during that revival, he got saved. He wanted to get married right away, so Bro. Kurtz could marry us.

Within a week, my mother made my wedding dress, and we got married on January 26, 1951.

Mickey has not slowed down since.

Three years after Mickey and I got married, he walked up in front of the church and said he was going to be a preacher. I said, "What?!"

I had married a meat cutter, not a preacher! I had said many times I would never marry a preacher. I grew up being in church every time the doors opened, and I knew what kind of life a preacher has - a hard life! Then when he announced he wanted to go to seminary, I really flipped.

First off, we loaded up and went to Louisiana. That was really my first time to be that far away from home. We lived right in the heart of New Orleans, and talk about culture shock! By the end of that year in New Orleans Seminary, we knew Mickey needed to go to college. So, once again, like a "good wife", I went with him.

Saying 'Good-bye' to "Our" Folks

When we got to Carson Newman College in Jefferson City, Tennessee, we had two children, Clint, and Dean who was only two months old.

Once again, I was a long way from home. It was cold. The baby cried all the time. We were in a little three-room house with an attic where Mickey would lock himself away to study his Greek and Homiletics. I would be downstairs with a crying baby - hour after hour. Most of the time after I fed him, he would immediately throw it back up.

I finally took Dean to a doctor and said, "You've got to do something with this baby, or I'm going to lose my mind."

The doctor put us in his car and drove to the hospital. He took x-rays of Dean and found he had a broken collarbone, which we think must have happened during birth because later on our youngest son, David, arrived in the same condition. It was such a blessing to find out what was causing his pain. He began to get better soon after the doctor put him in sort of a figure 8 sling. Later on, the folks at the church told us they had feared he

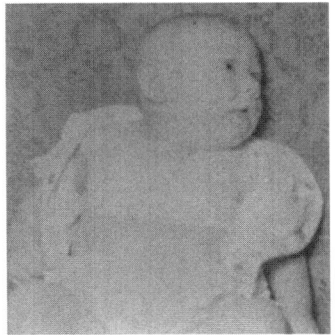

would die. Once again, God had proven His goodness to us. Just when we thought there was no hope of a solution, He stepped in and provided relief.

Every weekend we went to Washburn for Mickey to preach, and every time we made the trip over Clinch Mountain Road, Clint

Dean in Figure 8 Cast

and I would get carsick. Mickey would have to stop the car half way up at the same spot every time for us to get out and throw up.

The church people had a farmhouse for us to stay in on the weekends with a big wood stove for heat but no indoor plumbing. The outside privy had cracks in the walls that filled up with snow. Coming from Florida, I sure wasn't used to that. But once they accepted us -mountain folks take a while to feel you out – the graciousness and genuine love of the people in that little congregation more than made up for the accommodations.

Mickey was only making $28 a week, and I was making even less, but every weekend the folks of that church would load us up with fresh vegetables, milk, and meat, which really helped us out.

The only drawback was their milk cows would graze on those wild onions that grew on the sides of the mountain and you could smell and taste it in the milk.

They were used to it, but try as we might we just couldn't stomach it. Of course, we never refused it for fear of hurting their feelings, we would just pour it out for the neighbor's cat and bring back the empty bottle. One week the milk turned over in the car on the way home, and I thought we would never get the smell out.

Nevertheless, the strawberries they would give us were so good, they more than made up for the milk!

LM with Dean on the steps
of Washburn Baptist Church

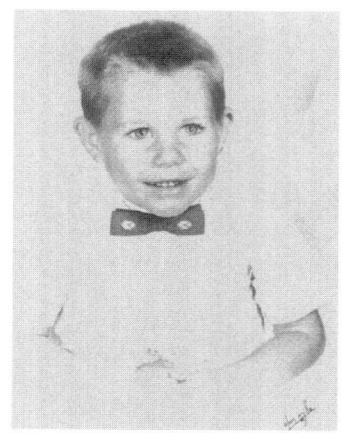
Dean Ernest Evans, born 1956.

We managed though. Carson Newman is a four- year school, but Mickey completed it in three and graduated summa- cum- laude. I got a PHT degree - Put Hubby Through!

As soon as *we* graduated, our little family packed up and headed south, back home to Okeechobee, boy was I ready to see my Mama and Daddy. Being an only child, we had always very close, and I had really missed them. So did Clint who was very fond of his grandpa, and even Mickey, who by now they loved as much as me, and had adopted as their own.

Chapter 3:

Mickey's Memories

Now, the story –

from the horse's mouth...

so to speak.

*"The Lord told me my childhood was preparation for
my life calling, but of course I didn't know that
whenI was living it."*

~ Mickey

I was born in Okeechobee, Florida in 1932. My parents, Albert and Edna Evans both drank heavily. They were alcoholics. They separated several times and finally divorced when I was twelve, so I never really knew my dad well. He must have been a smart man. He ran the Western Union for twenty-two years and could take a Morse code message and listen while I was bumming a nickel off him for a Coke. He liked poetry and recited it often.

Albert Allen Evans

I loved him.

But watching the things alcoholism did to my parents and the shame I lived with as a kid was part of my preparation.

Sixty years later, I buried a lady who was ninety-two years old, and I'd known her over fifty years. I preach a lot of funerals for the old-timers and their families, because I was part of that generation. I was the grandchild of Walkers, Raulersons, and Evans - all pioneer families who settled the Kissimmee Prairie with herds of free-ranging cattle. Mrs. Mellie Rose Raulerson had been the clerk for Brighton Baptist Church for many years, and at the funeral, they showed me the record of my having preached a revival at her church in 1954 - my first revival.

Following the church service, we went to the cemetery in Basinger to bury her. My father is buried there. My two sisters, my grandfather and my great grandfather, both in-laws - are all buried in the family plots under those ancient Live Oak trees.

As the other folks left, I lingered near my family plot. I felt a deep sense of loss. I sat down on a tombstone near my sisters' graves.   Louise and Margaret were their names. They both died right shortly after birth. I never had the chance to know my own sisters.

I thought about my dad and mourned the loss of him. He had held good jobs as a young man, but in his late forties fell deeper and deeper in his alcoholism.

When Laura Maye and I had been married for a couple years, I heard my father was living on skid row in Miami, and I had not heard from him in over a year.

I sent a letter to the Missing Person's Bureau in Miami to try to locate him. A few days later the Sheriff called me at work and said, "They found your daddy, and he's dead." Just like that. He was 51 years old. I went to Miami and found him in a morgue where they had done an autopsy on him.

That … was my father.

I made arrangements for an undertaker to pick him up, bring him home and embalm his ravaged body.

All those memories came flooding back to my mind that day after Mrs. Raulerson's funeral.   I had been plagued for fifty years, not knowing if my daddy was saved. I sat a long time. No matter that I am an old man, and my father has been dead many years - I am still his son who loves and misses him.

Finally I got in my truck, but I couldn't leave.

I prayed, "Lord, I want to ask you this: Was my daddy saved?"

Finally, the Lord spoke to me about it. "Don't grieve for your father anymore," He said. "Your father is with me, and your sisters are with me. They have grown into beautiful ladies." Such a sense of relief came over me. It was one of the greatest blessings I ever received from the Lord.

By the time I got to high school I was living alone in a twenty-five foot trailer and working for Sam Davis' Meat Packing Company.   Mr. and Mrs. Davis were devout Christians and were good to me. We went to work at three o'clock in the morning loading out the meat trucks. Then Mrs. Davis fixed a nice breakfast for me before taking me to school.   In the afternoon, they picked me up from school, and I went back to work. I also worked for my cousin Damon at his retail meat market.

I liked working. It helped me find my own identity, and it gave me a feeling of stability for the first time in my life. I began to dream about having my own meat business someday.

Laura Maye and I were sweethearts in high school. I had only dated two girls, and she was the second one. I sat behind her in English class and looked over her shoulder, so I could see her papers and pass the tests. I paid for that later when I got to college.

I wasn't even near to being a Christian when we started going together.   I smoked three packs of cigarettes and enjoyed playing poker on the weekends. Laura Maye was raised in church, and her folks were active members. They were not real happy about her dating a young man who wasn't saved, especially knowing my family background, (everyone in Okeechobee did) but they accepted me.

I was instructed however, that in order to take Laura Maye out, I would be expected at church first. So I complied just to be able to sit in the back row and watch her play that piano. Nonetheless, I was always the first one out the door, and I hated going to "dinners on the grounds" even more. I was way out of my element, not to mention my league, and I knew it.

After we graduated high school, Laura Maye went off to Jones Business College in Jacksonville. Things cooled off between us, but we kept in touch with letters and weekend dates when she commuted home on the train.

One weekend while she was home, an outside pastor had come to preach a revival at their church. I dutifully sat on the back row with the rest of the redneck cowboys who had also been drug there, just so I could take her out afterward, but a strange thing happened.

For the first time in my life, I heard the Gospel when the preacher actually made the audacious statement, *"God loves sinners. He hates sin, but He loves sinners!"* **I had never heard that before.**

Once, when I was a little boy, I was real sick. My father came and sat down on the bed to talk to me. He said, "Son, I want you to always be a good boy, because God has a big balance scale in Heaven. He puts your good deeds on one side and your bad deeds on the other. If your good outweighs the bad, you get to go to Heaven when you die."

He was trying to reassure me, give me good advice, I guess. But when he left the room I was terrified, because I was pretty sick and I thought, "I am going to die!" I was just a little fellow, but I knew if I had to balance the scales I would never make it. I didn't do the things I thought Christians did.

It scared me, and it stuck with me.

My parents didn't go to church, so I didn't either. In addition, I didn't have good "Sunday go-to-meetin clothes like people wore back then. Then once I lived on my own, the boys I ran around with didn't go to church. We played poker on Sunday. It was the only day I couldn't work because back then everything closed up on Sundays.

As I sat on the back row in Laura Maye's church that night, I thought, "This preacher is a fool. He doesn't know what he's talking about." I figured the deacons would get a hold of him and help straighten out his theology. In my infinite wisdom, I believed God only loved people who cleaned up nice and went to church on Sunday. I certainly knew I wasn't one of them. It *never* dawned on me that God could love somebody like me.

But it *was* an overwhelming idea, and I couldn't get it out of my head. I didn't understand it, but I went back the next night. And the preacher said it again. Every night he said it. I could not understand the deacons letting him get away with such heresy!

The third night it was like a light bulb came on in my mind. God loves sinners! I was a sinner! God loves me! When I got the thought through my head that God loves people like me, I responded to the invitation. Walking from the back row to the front, the Lord came into my heart. And I knew it!

I got saved, and I got a good dose of it. I immediately became an "evangelist," telling all my poker playing buddies how badly they needed religion. I had a lot of zeal but very little knowledge.

We had been married a short time, and I was working several jobs - in a slaughter house and a meat market. I was doing everything from rounding up cows, butchering them and cutting and packaging the meat. I was planning and working toward having my own wholesale meat business. In the middle of all my plans and work the Lord began to call me to ministry. I had no idea what that meant, because there had never been a preacher in my family. Ever!

I just knew I was supposed to do something for the Lord. I assumed that was to preach. I didn't know people could be called to do anything else. I preached my first sermon in 1952 in Brighton Baptist Church, a small, wooden building on the edge of the Seminole Indian Reservation. Within four of five minutes I had told the congregation everything I knew about the Bible. I was glad they had a pulpit so they couldn't see my knees shaking.

My first ministry was in the Okeechobee County Jail. My uncle, Louis Conrad, was the Sheriff, and he let me take the alcoholics out of jail on Sunday morning, drive them out to Brighton for church and bring them back to the jail in the afternoon.

Eventually, Laura Maye and I left the Brethren Church and joined the Baptist Church in Okeechobee. The Baptist had a younger crowd, and I was fired up and looking for where the fire was.

The funny thing was in order for us to become official members of First Baptist, of course you had to be baptized. Since I had already been baptized in Lake Okeechobee by the Brethren pastor, (in fact they believed in dipping you three times), I thought I was covered. Still the Baptists insisted I needed to be baptized

Mickey emerging from Lake Okeechobee after his first baptism

again in the church house baptismal. So now, I joke with people that it took four baptizings to clean me up!

We began having Bible studies in our home. Then they asked me to teach a Sunday school class for twelve-year-olds, and I quickly realized the kids knew more about the Bible than I did.

But I studied, and the kids taught me a lot.

When I went to the pastor to tell him that I knew the Lord had called me, but I didn't know what for, he said, "Well, if God has called you, it means he wants you to be trained. You need an education. I think you ought to go to school." Back then when people were "called to the ministry" it was just kind of assumed that meant becoming a preacher or a missionary.

I quit my jobs and sold the house.   Laura Maye and I packed up our son, Clint, and with my cousin, Damon Walker, Donald Burk and their families, headed off to Graceville Bible Institute in north Florida.

When we got to Graceville, the school turned our friend down Don, because his wife had been married before. He had not, but she had. We all agreed that was not right. If a man has been called, and he is sincere they should not refuse him an education in the ministry just because his wife had a previous marriage. So we left that school and Don and Juanita went on back to Okeechobee.

We were still packed up, so we just decided keep going and ended up at New Orleans Seminary. They offered a diploma course we could take. We didn't have money, so Laura Maye and I both got jobs. The only affordable apartment we could find was in the government housing projects for thirty dollars a month. It was a rough place to live. You couldn't even hang your laundry out on the line, without it disappearing. Clint's little tricycle got stolen right off the front steps. We had it pretty lean in those days and learned to live on less.

We met another seminary couple who were from Georgia. Reese and Laura Lee Sanders became some of our best friends. If they had food, they would share it with us, and when we had food, we would share it with them. I remember one night when neither of us had anything to share. We had pretty much resigned ourselves to going to bed hungry that night when we heard a knock on the door.

I still think the Lord sent an angel who was disguised as a sweet little Jewish lady, and in her hand she held out a huge artichoke. She said, "I have more of these than we can eat, and I thought you might could use one".

We thanked her gratefully, and walked back inside and looked at each other. None of us had never seen an artichoke before and had no idea how to go about cooking one. But Laura Maye and Laura Lee set about the task of making it edible and the four of us gratefully ate our first artichoke for supper that night.

Laura Maye worked in the daytime as a secretary, so I would out Clint in the nursery at school and attend classes all day. Then, when she got home, I would take two buses and a train to get across town to the supermarket where I worked as a meat cutter. It was a busy, but a good time.

I learned a lot about the Bible, but also about jail ministry and mission work in New Orleans. By the end of the year I realized just how ignorant I was, and knew I needed more education.

**Sonny Williamson
and Betty Chandler**

I enrolled at Carson Newman College in Jefferson City, Tennessee, and Laura Maye and I made plans to move up there. We came back to Okeechobee for the summer, and I worked for Buster Christopher who was a crop duster to save money to return to school. My job was to load the 500-pound hopper of the plane which usually made around 20 drops a day.

One of my uncles worked as a foreman on Frank Williamson's ranch. Frank's son, Frank Jr. (Sonny) and I grew up together. We were hunting, fishing, and dating buddies, so Mr. Frank Sr. knew me pretty well. One night just before we were ready to head back to school he invited me and Laura Maye to have supper with him.

He asked me if I was going back to school and I told him yes. He said, "I've been watching you grow up and saw you struggling to get your little meat business going. When you were ready, I was planning to back you in it. I was disappointed when you went into the ministry. But I see that you're sincere, and I want to help you with school. How much money you got?"

"I've got enough," I said. Which wasn't true. (You'd think I would have at least learned the Ten Commandments better after a year in seminary!)

Our second son Dean had been born, and we had spent

most of the money we had saved paying the hospital bill.

"Don't lie to me!" He said. "How much money you got?" I admitted I only had a couple hundred dollars. He said, "Well, how the Hell you think you're gonna go to school with that much money?"

"I will," I said stubbornly.

"I want to help you," he said.

"Mr. Frank, I can't do that. It's going to be three years before I can get out of school. I don't know when I can pay you back. I just don't want to do that."

"I ain't gonna loan you the money," he said. "Me and Laura Maye are gonna cut a deal, and you ain't got nothing to do with it. I want to learn how to play the piano, so when you get back from school I'm gonna take lessons from Laura Maye." I'm just gonna pay for my lessons early, by installments. He sent us one-hundred and fifty dollars a month – much more than piano lessons would have cost.

I carried twenty-one hours a semester, preached on the courthouse steps and the jail in Sevierville, and pastored Washburn Baptist Church over Clinch Mountain. That is where I really got my education. The mountain people shared everything they had with us and loved us. I gained invaluable experience and earned twenty-eight dollars every week.

Johnny and Idell Pearce

In 1958, we returned to Okeechobee. We arrived home on a Friday, and Monday morning I went to work on Johnny Pearce's ranch out by the Lake. We lived in a little house on the ranch that summer. It was a wonderful time for us. One day we were in working cows in the pens and the colt I was riding started to buck.

I was no bronc rider, and I hit the dirt pretty quick. As I was lying on the ground trying to catch my breath, a cow ran up and started hooking me. Jimmy Prescott ran her off me, then rode up and said "Get up there now Preacher, there's work to do and we ain't got time for you to be a takin no nap!" That's a lesson in Cowboy Philosophy – 101: anything that stops just short of killing you, is funny.

Laura Maye pregnant with David and Mickey happy living and working at the Pearce's place

In the fall, I got a little harder job teaching fourth grade in Okeechobee. Actually, I taught school two years in one - my first and my last! I have a lot of respect for schoolteachers! During that year, I also preached often out at Brighton, whenever Pastor Henry Sloan would let me, and continued doing jail and prison ministry.

Our family increased again with the birth of David Lee. So now we had three handsome boys and our family seemed complete. Or so we thought.

David Lee Evans, born 1958

I was working and hoping to make enough money to return to college. I wanted to go to Southwest Seminary in Texas to work on a doctorate.

Before we could make it to Texas, the people at Dunklin Memorial Baptist Church of Indiantown, led by our close friends Jack and Faye Williamson, called and asked me to be their pastor, and I accepted. One of my first projects as their pastor was to raise money to finish a large building they had started and were having trouble completing.

All of us men would go down there at night and work on the building together. Slowly the church began to grow. It wasn't a big church, but it was a healthy church.

After the church building was finished, we built a nice three-bedroom parsonage for our family next to the church. Laura Maye loved it. We both worked - she at the bank and I full-time as pastor of the church. I loved the people. They were good Cracker people, and we had a strong brotherhood among the men. I had no plans to ever leave. I thought it was my life calling.

Behind the pulpit at the Baptist Church in Indiantown

In 1959, Fidel Castro, overthrew the regime of Fulgencio Batista in Cuba. News of his filling the prisons with opposition forces reached us, and a retired Methodist minister, Arch Singletary, from Avon Park, FL began flying mission trips into Cuba to take relief materials and the Gospel to the men imprisoned by Castro.

I missed doing jail ministry, and I felt led to join him in this effort. So with the blessing of the church, we made several trips over to preach in prisons and with Laura Maye's parent's financial support, managed to set up a small church in the fishing village of Santa Spiritus.

I was sitting in a little shack eating supper with the

people who lived there, when Castro came on the radio and gave his first speech against America and announced he was a communist. Later, I was standing on a street corner when trucks loaded with Castro's troops came through town shouting in a frenzy, "Cuba si! Yankee no!"

After I got home, I made plans with another cowboy preacher/pilot, Jack James, for the following Saturday to fly our little Super-Cub over Havana and drop Bible tracts from the air.

As the end of the week approached, I got sick, was hospitalized with pneumonia, and missed my trip. A pastor from Miami took the mission, and his plane was shot down over Cuba. Castro's incessant campaign of slander against the United States, and nationalization of all American properties in Cuba halted our mission efforts to the island.

For nine years, I preached on a live radio program on Sunday nights at 11:30 on WOKC, Okeechobee. I finally decided one day there was nobody listening to me, so I didn't have to keep on with the radio program the rest of my life. I always had more zeal than wisdom and tried a little bit of everything.

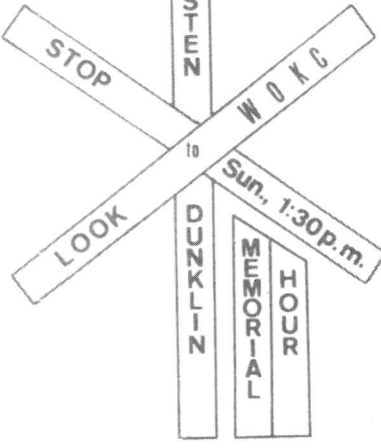

43

Chapter 4: The Vision

One night I was lying on the couch reading a book. I wasn't reading anything special. Just a book. All of a sudden, this vision came into my mind. I saw a little camp - not Dunklin as it is now - just a little camp.

I have always been a dreamer - projects going on in my brain all the time. Most people do.

But this was different. I knew it wasn't my idea. The Spirit of the Lord was so strong and came all over me. The experience was so powerful that I lay awake all night in awe of what I saw in my mind. I kept asking, "What is the camp for, Lord?" Finally, the Lord said to me, "The camp is for alcoholics to come to for help."

At daylight, I woke Laura Maye and told her. She probably thought I had dreamed it and went back to sleep. I didn't know what to do, but I knew it was God. Every night it came back. The same thing. I couldn't sleep for this vision burning in my heart.

I thought, okay, I'll take some men from the church, and we'll go out in the woods somewhere, build a little camp, and hire somebody to run it. I thought the camp was a good idea.

But then the Lord said, "No, I want *you* to do it. I want you to leave the church. I want you to work full- time on building the camp."

I had more fear than faith as I did my best to convince the Lord that He had made a mistake... had sent the message to the wrong man. I reminded Him how well things were going in the Church, how much my family was enjoying our new parsonage. Besides, I didn't have money to build anything.

I fought hard, wrestling with God for two months before surrendering to His call. That was in the spring of 1962.

During the time I had the vision, I was preaching a series of messages in the church about walking by faith, quoting from Hebrews 11:8-9 *"By faith Abraham, when he was called to go out into a place which he should after receive for an inheritance, obeyed; and he went out, not knowing whither he went. By faith he sojourned in the land of promise, as in a strange country, dwelling in tabernacles with Isaac and Jacob, the heirs with him of the same promise."* But little did I dream that God would call me to practice what I was preaching. It was a frightening experience to actually be the one "not knowing whither he went."

Laura Maye: We had been at the church in Indiantown five years and had just moved out of the roach infested parsonage into a brand new one. I had three kids by that time, Clint, Dean and David and was also working at the local bank.

Then Mickey just comes waltzing in one morning and says, "Honey, I had a vision. We're going to go out in the woods and start a camp for alcoholics." Now you have to remember that I had never been around drinking or alcoholics. I did not know anyone in my family who drank. So this was going to be a new experience for me. In fact, the first time I had ever even seen anyone getting drunk was on our Senior Skip day down in Key West where our coach provided enough margarita mix to get the whole class drunk – and mixed it up in a bath tub!

But I told myself not to worry too much.

I thought he'd get over it.

He did not get over it.

Mickey: My first problem was I didn't know where to build this camp. I just knew I was supposed to do it. I was still pastoring the church. One morning I went in the little restaurant in Indiantown to drink coffee with the other men who stopped by. Harold Douglas and a couple of other cowboy friends, Donald and Martin Brown, were in there, and I told them I was looking for a little piece of land to build a camp on for alcoholics.

One of them said, "Well, one of the prettiest hammocks in this county is on my daddy's ranch." Fox Brown owned a good-sized ranch, several thousand acres, but he had sold two sections of it to a Jewish man from New York. So I headed out to check on this piece of land.

Harold and I took Fox Brown Road out from Indiantown. It was seven miles of dirt road, and we had to stop at every fence, get out and open and close a gate. We finally reached 714, got out and climbed through the barbwire fence. We walked the property.   I stood there looking around and felt this was it. This was the right place to build the camp.

I found the real estate man who was handling the deal. He told me the Jewish man was willing to sell the land, but I would have to get a release from Fox Brown stating that he would agree to sell me part of it. The least he could sell would be a half section.

I asked, "What does he want for it?" "He wants $200 per acre. That's $64,000," he said. "You go see Fox Brown, and ask if he'll release the deed."

I didn't have sixty-four cents, but I drove back out that dirt road, and I recognized Mr. Brown's truck meeting me. We were both going slow, because the road was rough. I flagged him down, and we stopped in the road to talk. I said, "Mr. Brown, I understand you own the mortgage on this piece of property up here. I want to buy a piece of it."

"What do you want it for?" He asked.

I told him about my plans to build a camp for alcoholics to come to for help.

He asked, "You got any money?" I said, "No, sir."

He said, "Well, how the hell you think you're gonna buy it with no money?" He was an old moonshiner himself and he wasn't about to cut me any slack.

I said, "Well, sir, I really believe the Lord is telling me to do this, and if the Lord is in it, I believe he will provide the money."

He thought about that for a minute and began to bargain with me. "If you'll sell me back twenty acres of it for my daughter for the same price you pay for it, then I'll release it for you... *If* the Lord gives you any money, that is."

So I went back to the real estate man and told him what Fox Brown had said. He agreed to contact the buyer from New York and present him my offer. "But," he said, "the man has recently moved to France. I'll have to track him down. And before he'll even pay attention to you, you got to put up some earnest money."

I said, "Mister, I'm the most earnest man you ever saw, but I don't have any money." He said, "Well, you need to put up at least $3000." That was a lot of money for a man who was making $75 per week. I left the real estate office wondering where I was going come up with that kind of money. It would certainly have to be the Lord's doing. A few nights after my meeting with the real-estate man, Norman Hales came to my house.

He owned a dairy near Indiantown. He was an alcoholic, and I had often gone out to witness to him and the men he had working for him. He had never been to our house before, so I was surprised to see him.

He said, "Mickey, I heard you mention something about a mission you are gonna build." I thought he was referring to our project in Cuba. I began explaining what happened to our work there, and he stopped me. "No, no I don't mean Cuba," he said. "I mean this place you're gonna have for drunks."

I said, "Well, I found the land. I'm just waiting on the Lord to show us what to do." He said. "I wish you had it now, Mickey. I'm drinkin a quart of liquor a day, and I need what you're talkin about. I want to help you a little bit with it." He pulled out a check already made out for $3000. I almost fell over.

I took it straight to the real estate man and said, "Here. I'm still earnest, and now I've got some money." That was the deposit, but we still needed the balance of the $64,000.

I remember feeling very alone in those days. I tried desperately to share my vision with my family and close friends, but it was hard for them to see what existed only as a dream in my mind. But slowly the Lord began to touch people's hearts, and one by one, they began to catch the vision as well.

"The first time I met Mickey, he seemed to have an uncanny ability to feel what other people felt and to share their hurts. He had the strongest desire to do something to lift their lives and heal their suffering. Hurting people are especially drawn to him because of that. Mickey's compassion, together with his salvation, calling to ministry and the wife he chose, Laura Maye - put all those things together, and a miracle was bound to happen. He loves people, and they can tell it. People understand compassion and humility and respond to it. All of us have these

qualities, more or less, but some of us get serious about them and others pass over them. But every once in a while a person comes along who communicates that compassion and lives that vision – and that is a marvel to behold. One day he called me, and said God had told him to go out in the wilderness, buy a place and build a camp for alcoholics. Just like that. It didn't bother him that he didn't have a thousand dollars to even start. He just knew that he was supposed to do it. He knew he was supposed to do what God told him to do.

That is the miracle of Mickey. Anyway, that day he called, his manner told me I needed to get on the train, because it was leaving the station. Indeed it did."

Frank(Sonny)Williamson Jr.,
Close Friend and Member
of First Board of Directors
with his wife Betty, and
children Kim, Wes and Karen.

Then things began to happen.

The Lord moved on Laura Maye's mother and father to sell their house and twenty acres in Okeechobee, and use the money to purchase the mortgage for the Camp. The Lord had indeed made a way in the wilderness, and the property would be dedicated to Him.

LM in front of her parent's home.

Chapter 5:
The Reality

We got in the car, and I drove Laura Maye out to see the land. She wasn't happy about all the gates and potholes in the dirt road we had to go through to get there. Finally we arrived, and I held up the fence for her to climb through. We waded through weeds waist deep out toward the giant oak trees and grape vines as thick as my arm. I had been out there several times at this point and could already envision the camp. I said, "Honey, this is going to be a wonderful -we'll build the dorms here, the kitchen over there ..." Wouldn't you know, about that time she stepped on a big blacksnake and it wrapped itself around her leg. She stomped and jumped around and finally got rid of it. I teased her after that about clearing the first three acres all by herself!

When we first got the land, there was nothing here but a dipping vat for cattle. We would camp out there on the weekends and work on the property.

In order to keep things afloat financially, I would preach revivals around Florida - eighteen that first year. The first of those was in Adrian Rogers's church at Ft. Pierce. It was there I met a man with the same tenacity as Brother Dunklin. Adrian had asked me to mention the Camp, and tell what it was all about. I maybe talked five minutes about the vision and building this camp for alcoholics. A few days after the service, a man named Al Cross came to see me. He introduced himself and said, "God told me to go help you build this camp." I said, "Well, Al, I'd love to have you, but I don't have any money to pay you." He just replied, "The Lord didn't say anything about money. He just said to go help you."

I asked what he did for a living. He told me that he had been with the State Road Department for twenty years. I said, "Well, Al, if you quit now, you'll lose your retirement." Al flatly stated, "God didn't say anything about retirement. He just said to go and help you, and that's what I aim to do."

So, Al Cross became our first staff member. He was a recovered alcoholic himself, and was a living testimony to the men, showing them what God could do with a surrendered life. He served here faithfully for eighteen years.

Al Cross Teaching Class

Every year at Homecoming, I would ask Al to close out the last service by singing Amazing Grace. He could really belt it out. A short time before he died of cancer I went to visit him at the VA hospital in St. Petersburg. I told him "Al you need to get better and get on up out of this bed so you can lead us in Amazing Grace this Homecoming." He said "Mickey, I don't know if I'm gonna make it to Homecoming this year, but if I don't, I'll make you a deal. I'll gather up all the alumni in heaven, and we'll join yall in the last stanza from up there. Al didn't make it to Homecoming at Dunklin that year. The Lord took him on to Heaven. So as we sang "when we've been there ten thousand years, bright shining as the sun, we've no less days to sing His praise than when we first begun" the congregation looked up toward Heaven and we all waved to Al and all the other alumni who had passed on to the other side, and that has been our tradition at Homecoming ever since.

After that Austin would lead us in "I'll Fly Away" and we'd all feel like we'd touched heaven.

Reba and Al Cross

AL's TESTIMONY

I was thirty-three years old and drunk. I had been drinking for seventeen years - over half my life, and the last five years I had been a severe alcoholic.

I had lost my driver's license, was in debt, had been in jail several times, and had almost lost my job.

A few hours before daylight on the morning of February 1, 1960, somebody picked me up and took me to see my mother, who had suffered a stroke and wasn't expected to survive.

I knelt by her bed and asked God for help. I asked God to save me and to take all desire for alcohol from me, and he did. My mother also rallied and lived another three years.

I had my own personal experience with Bro. Dunklin when I was a small child.

The old preacher was walking by our house while my mother was hanging out the laundry. When the clothesline broke and the hand-scrubbed clothes fell to the ground, my mother angrily verbalized her frustration.

Brother Dunklin walked up and quietly started helping her pick up the wet clothes, and repair the clothesline. I was just a toddler sitting in a clothesbasket at the time, but my mother often retold the story of how Bro. Dunklin led her to the Lord that day and dedicated me to the Lord's work.

It was in the fall of 1963, that I first came to help Mickey at Dunklin Memorial Camp. That is about all there was to the place - a name. A fellow who came out here with me asked, "Did you say this place was out IN the country or out OF the country?"

I did become aware of two strong things here on this swampy piece of land: the Spirit of God, and Mickey's belief in his vision. If I was to stay and become a part of this ministry, I must believe too.

When the first man came into the program, he was in bad shape from an extended drinking episode. Mickey had to be in a meeting the first night, so that left me alone with the man.

After he went to sleep I got on my knees and asked God to do for him what He had done for me. I wanted to see God start us off with a victory.

The next morning when I got up the man was gone.   I was disappointed.

Then I heard a noise out in front of our cabin. The man was playing with our two dogs. He had been out hunting with them. I watched as he came in, spoke to me, and started fixing breakfast. After breakfast I asked him how he felt about this drinking business, and he said, "I don't want to have anything else to do with it." He never did.

**Our Two Beagle Hounds , named "Cash" and "Credit"
looking for some payment**

David "camping out" at the Camp

Laura Maye: "We all pitched in and things started to slowly come together. Before I knew it, I had been moved out of my new parsonage in town and into a tar paper shack (Mickey called it a cabin or 'fishing cottage' - I called it a shack) out in the middle of nowhere."

Actually, it was two "cottages". The boys slept in one and we slept in the other.   We were still cooking outside, but at least we didn't have to sleep in the tent. Eventually we built a room between the two and just kept adding rooms as we could, until we eventually had it turned into a real "house".

Lily Nix and Laura Maye preparing meals for the men

Momma and Daddy believed in the vision so much so, that they sold their land and home in Okeechobee and became the first full time volunteers at the Camp living their remaining years here. They moved out in an Airstream trailer and built a house around it that is still here today next to the Rec Hall.

Ernest and Stella Campbell

The old Airstream as it appears today

One day Al Cross was burning brush up on the north end of the property, and the fire got away from him. A stiff wind came up and was pushing it right through the cabbage woods toward the Camp. The fire department was here. The men and the staff were all fighting the fire.

We began to think we were going to lose the whole Camp.

My mother was a prayer warrior. She started praying, and five minutes later, the wind suddenly changed, and the Lord saved our buildings. That fire continued to burn on another four days - all the way to the railroad tracks, but not one of our structures was touched.

Besides keeping the Camp covered in prayer, Momma mended the men's clothing, made quilts to sell, shelled peas …. whatever needed to be done.

My Daddy had a knack for growing things. He started raising calves, hogs, and meat rabbits for the Camp. He also had a green thumb and always planted a big garden.

Dean, Evans, Pa Campbell and David Evans

He even built worm beds in the woods behind their house, and planted all those vines you see growing on the trees to shade them. He used the castings to fertilize the garden and sold the crawlers that didn't end up on his hook (he loved to fish) to the bait shops. He tried to raise chickens, but the coons and foxes always figured out a way to get them. Finally, he gave up, and even made one of the coons a pet. If you live here, you can blame him the next time one gets into your garbage can.

Pa Campbell feeding pet coon

Chapter 6: The Inspiration

Reverend E.M.C. Dunklin

Many folks over the years have asked where the name for the camp came from. Brother Dunklin was a circuit preacher assigned to the Everglades region by the Baptist Association. The Seminole Indians affectionately dubbed him "The Little Jesus Man". His faith and compassion for all people was evident as he traveled through the swamps and hammocks around Lake Okeechobee.

When he came to the region in 1921, he traveled mostly by foot. The land was extremely rough to travel, being under populated by people, and overpopulated by gators and snakes. When dark came, if Bro. Dunklin wasn't near a home, he simply unrolled his blankets and slept on the ground.

Eventually he acquired a horse, which he hoped would help him reach more people. But it also presented him with the problem of caring for the animal. Once a reluctant host complained that it was bad enough that he had to feed a preacher, but now also had to feed the preacher's horse! To which   Bro. Dunklin replied, "Feed the horse and let the preacher go hungry."   The man and his family were shortly afterward baptized. Brother Dunklin was a man who knew how to walk out what he talked about.

"When I (Mickey) was five, Brother Dunklin visited our home and according to his custom prayed for our family. He placed his hands on my head and asked God to bless and use me in His service.   Ever after, when I saw him coming, I would climb up in the cherry tree in our back yard, and pick cherries for him to eat. He liked those big, black cherries."

The commercial catfish fishermen and cowboys all took off their hats and reverently bowed their heads, when Bro. Dunklin would come into the local watering holes where they drank, played poker and fought. He didn't preach at them. He always asked them about their families, and how things were going. When he got ready to leave, he'd take his hat off and say, "Boys, let's have a word of prayer. "

Grown men have cried when they related stories about his visits to the saloons in the frontier days of Okeechobee.

I wanted everyone to remember the work the Lord had done through him, so we named the Camp after him. His great-granddaughter, Judge Carolynn Parr, pictured here with her husband Jerry, inherited Bro. Dunklin's missionary spirit, and they have supported the Camp in his honor.

Jerry and Carolyn Parr

God's Little Deputy

From the frontier Florida town
of Okeechobee years ago,
Comes a story almost legend,
but still many don't know.
It's a heartwarming story
Of the courage, faith, and love
Of a backwoods pioneer preacher
Who was led by God above
He had come to this wild country
with a vow that he would tame
the lawless breed who lived here;
Brother Dunklin was his name.
To this cruel and ruthless country,
fraught with hardship and distress
He had come to build a chapel
in the untamed wilderness.
With no fear of death within him
And the only will "Thy Will be done,"
Dunklin taught the Law of Moses,
where the law was each man's gun.
Here among the wicked outlaws
one and all the Devil's breed,
God's faithful little servant,
Carried on his holy deed.
With the Light of God to lead him
and the Bible in his hands.
He had vowed to bring salvation
to this untamed Satan's band.
Through the years, he preached the Gospel
Through the day and through the night
On the streets and in the bars
Or in the homes by dim lamplight
For to him, it made no difference,
 And whatever need was shown
Brother Dunklin made an altar
where the Word of God was known.

None can count his deeds of kindness
Nor the many miles he trod
Helping those who, lost in blindness,
Sought the healing Hand of God
Many souls he won for Jesus
And in God's own Holy Name
He installed the Ten Commandments
 into hearts, no law could tame.
Twenty years he struggled onward
 in the cruel and Godless town;
Never did he dare to falter
Lest he let the Lord's work down
And then one day the tired old man
could see his work was done,
the lawlessness had faded
and a change had begun
And his heart was filled with gladness
As he left this conquered land
Much the same way he had come here
With a Bible in his hands
He had come to this wild country,
Braved the hardships and distress;
He had come and built a chapel
In the untamed wilderness
In later years the word came back
That Dunklin had passed away...
Many an old pioneer's heart
hurt on that sad day.
And in the words of one of those
"When Dunklin died the world lost a friend,
but God gained a deputy."

Chapter 7:

A Table Prepared in the Wilderness

Isa. 35:1 ... "The wilderness and the solitary place shall be glad for them; and
the desert shall rejoice, and blossom as
the rose." Through God's sunshine and
rain and Pa and Thomas's planting and
cultivation, fresh vegetables will soon
grace our table here!

. As the Camp family grew, God was always faithful to supply our needs. Our local farmers ranchers and fisherman have always been very generous to share their crops, cattle and catches with the Camp. In addition to supplying immediate needs for food, they have also supported the Camp's own efforts to cultivate sustainable food production to meet the needs of the expanding population, and generate a surplus for revenue. As seed stock and equipment were donated - gardens, groves, and pastures were planted.

"Them turnips is good pickin's". D.M.C. garden

Farming has always been an integral part of Dunklin over the years, from raising dairy calves to a crossbred beef herd, from a citrus grove to gift fruit packing plant, feedlot, the Camp produces our own hay and feed in a homemade feed mill. The following are a few of the excerpts and pictures from early editions of the "Camp Blessings" articles written by Mickey in the newsletter each month documenting the Lord's provisions.

"We are very grateful to Bro. Frank Tillis for sending us two truckloads of black-eyed peas for our canning plant and 100lbs of seeds for our garden. Frank apologized that the three rows of ham hocks he planted didn't come up.

Bro. Tillis also donated a new freezer door, and J.S. Barwick furnished Styrofoam for the insulation in the new walk in vegetable   freezer we are building.

Thank you to Strickland Egg Farm, who donated hens which were delicious, cooked with dumplings.

The cattle are not only fed out to provide meat in the cooler, but the surplus are sold to provide the "grits 'n gravy" to go with the meat."

We have been blessed By Dr. Nelson Makinson, Dr. Frank Platt and Dr. Jim Harvey who have performed countless hours of volunteer veterinary work on our livestock.

Dr. Makinson, and Roy

Hubert Waldron (on right) oversaw our cattle herd for many years. That was a man who had forgotten more about cattle than I will ever know. He also had a little butcher shop behind his house where he cut meat for family and friends. He and his wife, Vivian, were just good, salt of the earth, kind of people. She made the best sweat tea in all of Okeechobee. When Hubert retired Glen Bass stepped in and ran the operation for us. Elda Maye and all the Bass family have been a blessing. Another one of the old ranching families who helped us out a whole lot were Norman and Alma Stokes. Norman was one of the toughest men I have ever had the privilege to know. He came from pioneer stock and even though we were close in age, I considered him a mentor. Miss Alma still works their place, now with their grandchildren carrying on the heritage.

Along with the cattle, which were the main source of income, we also raised and sold ornamental plants, grew citrus, made cypress knee furniture, ran a retail bookstore, and held carwashes. Pretty much anything we could think of to help pay the bills and put food on the table. Wayne and Mike Cole donated a large industrial baking oven and taught Red how to make bread. We would load up the van and go sell bread around Okeechobee. Uncle Lawrence and Aunt Nancy Rhoden made jelly and syrup that was mighty tasty on that homemade bread.

Lawrence and Nancy Rhoden

Our dream of starting an ornamental nursery at the Camp has become a reality over night by the generosity of Mr. Roy Rood from the Rood Landscaping Co. at Jupiter, Florida. Roy has provided us with fifteen different varieties of ornamental plants to field-plant and to stock our outlet store.

Mr. Homer Wall at the W & W Lumber Company at Indiantown has provided space for our Retail Outlet and Jack Phipps is handling the sales for us.

Mr. "Doodles" Williams from Miami gave us over 600 beautiful bottle brush plants to landscape the new property.

The income from our nursery project helps toward the development of the Laos Institute. It will enable some of our men to recieve further training beyond the rehabilitation program.

The only annual organized "donation drive" we have ever promoted is our Yearling-a-Year program, where cattlemen were implored to either donate a heifer to our herd or earmark the proceeds from sale a calf at the market to DMC.

We learned valuable lessons of faith as we literally looked to the Lord for our daily bread. The staff, our boys, and the men, worked side-by-side to clear land, plant the pastures, gardens and orange groves. We raised dairy calves, rabbits, sheep and hogs for meat and grew our own vegetables.

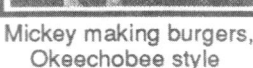
Mickey making burgers, Okeechobee style

One of the first permanent buildings to be erected at Dunklin was the butcher shop. I had been a meat cutter by trade and those skills came in handy for use at the Camp in making provisions for the men and families.

The canning plant, bakery and north kitchen were added later to further assist the Camp in being as self supportive foodwise as possible. The goal has always been to produce enough meat, vegetables and fruit on site to not only supply the needs at Dunklin, but to have enough share with other ministries as well. With this due diligence and the Lord's blessing no one at Dunklin has ever had to miss a meal – unless they were fasting! In fact, most of the men attest to the abundance of God's faithfulness by gaining and average 15-20 extra "Dunklin pounds" while going through the program.

Clint and Grandpa pouring fertilizer

The Lord faithfully provided ways for us to gather not only daily bread, but meat for special occasions as well. One Christmas day, Laura Maye's daddy and I went out in the hammock and killed fifty squirrels for our dinner.

The Lord's manna always fell on us in interesting forms. Our second anniversary Thanksgiving meal was a wild turkey Laura Maye killed on the grade with her car, supplemented by an oven full of donated wild mallard ducks shot the day before on a game farm down the road. A wealthy but generous heiress who lived on Palm Beach Island, liked to fly her friends out in a helicopter to hunt on the weekends. Every time we heard that helicopter go overhead, we knew ducks were soon to drop.

LM and Duck-copter pilot

George Washington (standing) and company plucking wild ducks)

Potato #624
Just Like The Army!!

Bro. Jimmy Hinkle from Shiloh Youth
Ranch shares a load of canned vegetables with us.

Many times the Lord blessed us through the generosity
of other ministries and churches. As we have grown, we
believe it is an important part of our mission to "pay it
forward" and support other ministries in both financial
and practical ways. For a time, we ran cattle in
conjunction with Faith Farm. The combined crew is
shown below.

Dwayne Heaberlin, Glen Bass, Chicky Evans, John and Sandi Glenn,
and Kim Bullard saddle up together.

Clifford Bennett

Clifford and Josephine Bennett cooked many a pot of swamp cabbage and pan of cathead biscuits for Dunklin gatherings. They drove all the way from Basinger each week to attend church and volunteer their services. Their children Johnny, Cindi, David, Marci, Missy and Allen were all part of the Camp family and two of Clifford's brothers went through the program .

ph Bennett on right

Josephine canning black eyed peas

Leslie Bennett and Austin Brown

Another tradition that began early on, and is still practiced at Dunklin today is the making of old fashioned cane syrup. The process is a nearly lost art that has been passed down through the generations starting with Thomas Nix and continued by Lawrence Rhoden and

Thomas Nix grinding cane

Ormond Simmons then Freeman Nettles, who passed the

Ormond Simmons and
Lawrence Rhoden

skills on down to Chris Bryan. At one time the Canal Point Agricultural Experimental Station would send 500 gallon tanks of cane juice which would be cooked down into syrup in an iron kettle that is still being used nearly 50 years later. The raw cane is grown on site, harvested and made into syrup keeping this unique Florida Cracker tradition intact for the next generation.

Thomas Nix and John Thomas
dipping the syrup

Zeke and Chris Bryan
skimming the juice

Chapter 8:
"Critters... invited and otherwise"

By 1965, we had twenty-six hogs, twenty-five head of cattle, two sheep, six horses, a slew of rabbits, assorted ducks, chickens, sheep, a goat, a half dozen dogs and an assortment of pets including a kinkajou. We even had a sea lion seal. Gene Black caught it near his fish house in Salerno, when it swam up to their dock. He offered to bring him out to the Camp. Trying to politely decline the offer, I told Gene the lake did not have enough fish to support the seal, (which was true), but Gene insisted that since he already hauled out a couple hundred pounds of fish a week for the fish fry, he would just bring a few more with him for our new pet.

Sam was friendly, and would come out of the water and right up to anyone he thought might feed him. Not everyone realized he was gentled though, and one day, one of my good friends, who shall remain nameless,

SAM our newest Pet

was treed by Sam, before he realized the beast was just looking for a treat. We called the sea lion Sam, but we never actually knew for sure if it was a Sam or Samantha.

Cleaning fish for Friday Night

A man showed up at the Camp one day with a cow, some ducks, and a monkey in a horse trailer. He said we could have them if we wanted them. I told him we could certainly use the cow, and we could always eat the ducks, but I didn't have any use for a monkey. He said, "Well, if you don't take the monkey, you cain't have the rest!" So, the camp had a monkey.

It was an odd sight – seeing a monkey swinging through the trees in the middle of a Florida swamp. Some of the men who hadn't been detoxed very long thought they were going back into D.T.'s and hallucinating, upon seeing the monkey for the first time. Then when they were just about sobered up, Sam the seal would run them up a tree.

Dean with puppy and "Monk"

Nobody liked the monkey except Dean and Laura Maye. In fact, Al said the monkey had to be demon possessed to cause as much trouble as he did. Sometimes that monkey unscrewed light bulbs and dropped them on the ground.

Laura Maye was doing laundry one day on a ringer washer outside. She went in the house to get something. Hearing a commotion out at the washhouse, she ran back outside only to find the monkey with only his head sticking through the wringer. His entire body had gone through the rollers. Then there was the time he got a hold of her lipstick and marked all over the walls of the house…

Another day she was hosting a picnic lunch for a group of WMU ladies who had quilted blankets for the men. She didn't realize the monkey was in an oak tree overhead until he proceeded to begin emptying airplants filled with buggy brown water down onto the heads of the fashionable ladies below.

Notice the high efficiency washer and dryer

 He loved to climb the clothesline, unpin the wet laundry, and watch with glee as the white sheets fell to the mud below.

Finally, he went too far with Laura Maye.

He got in the house, into the medicine cabinet and got a box of ExLax. You know - the kind that used to come in those little bars like chocolate? She chased him out, and he scampered up on top of the house, where he proceeded to open the box and eat the whole thing with a grin on his face, seeming to savor every bite. He knew he had gotten away with something, but he didn't know the surprise he was in for. Later that night, he climbed in her car to relieve himself, and that was the end of their friendship.

Chapter 9:

Focus on Family & Friends

Laura Maye: "Mickey will tell you when he moved us out to Dunklin, the Devil tried to convince him that our family would starve to death, but it's been the total opposite – we've all struggled with obesity!

I didn't worry about my boys being around alcoholics, but I was concerned about them being out here with no other children to play with. Mickey made them work just like the men. We had friction over that many times. At one point, I was ready to take the boys and leave it with him."

Clint, Laura Maye, David and Dean Evans

David spending another summer planting grass

Laura Lee Evans, born 1971

By the time Lauralee came along fourteen years after David, things were a bit more established, so it was a lot easier on her than it had been for her brothers.

Over the years, Mickey has tried to make it up to the boys, but they each have had to deal with their own issues stemming from the hard way they were raised at the Dunklin. We were too far out for them to be involved in most extracurricular activities or sports, and the main thing here for them was work. And there was always plenty of it needing to get done. That's one of the major drawbacks of living where you work.

The work is always there staring you in the face, and it s hard to really be "off" and relax with so much needing to be done.

It takes a toll on the staff and their families, although today's staff seem better at setting those healthy boundaries. I pray they have learned from our mistakes. The only boundaries we knew about back then were the kind that marked off land.

Amazingly, each of our children have come back to work for the Camp at various times Clint is a great photographer. He developed the Camp's first video productions and Nancy

worked in our office. They now live in Palm Harbor. He works in the medical software field, and she works with an attorney. They have two grown children.

A daughter, Amanda Lee ,who is married to Frank Seaton

Clinton Ira, who works with Florida Fish and Wildlife

The Alvarez Family

Julie and Delton Lynch, Ira, Chicky and Jennifer Evans, Amanda and Frank Seaton, Nancy and Clint Evans, Connie "Minnie" and TiTi Alvarez.

Dean developed our medical clinic, and oversees the ongoing renovation of Prayer Island. He and his wife, Rosalia Leite-Evans, live in West Palm Beach and both work in the medical field.

We lost our grandson, Dean's son, Christopher to suicide in 2008.

The Prayer Island renovations are dedicated in part to his memory.

David Evans, son of the founder of DMC, works in the butcher shop with his wife, Chicky.

David and Chicky- who happens to be Nancy's sister - ran the slaughterhouse operation for over fifteen years. Chicky is right up there in the ranks with Red Fox when it comes to being able to fix just about anything. Her father had worked as a mechanic for the city of Tampa for many years and taught her well. When David and Chicky had our first grandchild, Jennifer, Red Fox quipped that the real reason Chicky had gotten pregnant was to show the men she could do something that they couldn't!

Later, David went back to college and Chicky continued to cut meat. He earned a technical degree and went to work at Florida Power & Light until they were both injured in a boating accident.

David and Chicky have one daughter, Jennifer Lynn, who is an Environmental Specialist with Saint Lucie County.

Being raised in Tampa, it was a leap of faith Nancy and Chicky took to marry our boys and move out here to the boonies. They have both been so faithful to our family, and also the mission of Dunklin through the years.

EXTENDED FAMILY

Grandson Christopher and my Aunts Christine Campbell and Corene Gieger are among the family waiting for us in Heaven.

Not Pictured: Betty, Amber, Kevin and Cindy Gordon

Tuff Marsh, Tammy & JR Booker

Rick and Kim Trask

Son-in-law Chris with cousin Gwen Marsh

Corene Geiger and Gary Marsh

Lauralee and her husband Chris Bryan live at Dunklin
with their son Zeke.

Chris is foreman over the
Camp's ranch operations.
Our boys helped us plant
the pastures, and now
Zeke helps his daddy bale
hay off those same fields. I
guess things have come
full circle.

Now, back to the beginning...

When we first started the Camp there was no bus coming out here to take the kids to school. The school board told me that if I wanted my kids to ride a bus, I would have to drive it myself and pick up the other kids along the way. I'll tell you, never in my life would I have dreamed this is what I would have been doing at 30 years old. So, at 5:30 every morning I found myself driving a school bus on the Grade. Then coming back to the Camp in the evening and driving a tractor to plant grass. It was so muddy at the camp we often had to pull the bus out to the road with the tractor! The first time I got in that bus and looked in the mirror to the back, it looked a hundred feet long. The roads were not paved and were horrible. Nearly every week I'd break down. When they started paving the 714 from the crossroad toward Stuart, I'd have to go through that every day. I'd get stuck, and someone would come along and pull me out. I think the school district gave me the worst bus, too.

One time I ran over something and one of the kids yelled, "Ms. Evans you ran over something back there – maybe somebody!" I threw the bus in park and ran to investigate. It was a dog I had run over.

The last day I drove the bus the hood fell off somewhere down the road, and I just left it. I'd had it. I drove that bus to the school and said, "If you want the hood it's out there. I'm done!"

When Al Cross heard about me getting mad and quitting my bus-driving job, he teased me saying, "It's a sorry woman who can't even support seventeen men." There were about fifteen in the program at that time, plus Al and Mickey.

Al Cross, LM, David, Dean, Mickey and unknown
man planting grass

Mickey: Before there were phone lines this far out, our only way of communication at the Camp was by two-way CB radio. Phone calls would come in to Matson Dairy would receive our calls and then relay them to us by the two-way radio. Then FCC changed the frequency, and rendered it inoperable. The receptions got so tangled up, that you could hear people in south America better than at the dairy, which was ten miles away. Allapatah's folks were the first to receive phone service, so they would let us come down there to make calls. During the interim years, between when the CB went down, and the phones lines reached us there was no way to communicate on-site. When the phone lines did reach us, we were on a "party line" with all the other folks, which gave a different twist to "call waiting".

The only other houses on the grade from the 4-way crossing were on Carlton and Allapattah Ranches. The roadway was dirt all the way into town. There was a place on the Palm City end that had a high aluminum fence all the way around it. We had learned through the grapevine that it was a nudist colony. Brother Al broke down one night right in front of it, but he was too embarrassed to go and ask to use the phone, so he slept in the car all night.

Laura Maye: I was teaching in marriage class on a Sunday afternoon, and I was finishing when somebody rushed in and said, "Laura Maye, you need to come! Mickey's been in an airplane accident!" I said, "No way! What are you talking about?!" It had been less than a year since he had crashed his plane over at Venus.

I couldn't imagine Mickey climbing in the plane with her. She had just gotten her license and had flown in and offered him a ride. He wanted to prove to himself that he wasn't afraid to fly again, so he pulled his back brace off and got in the plane.

We got in the car and rushed out to the airstrip. The first thing I saw was this little plane wrapped around a tree. It looked like it was made of matchsticks and paper. During takeoff, a hard gust of wind puffed across the dirt runway. The pilot lost control, and the plane crashed into a pine tree. It actually looked like a worse crash than the earlier one Mickey had been in where he broke his back, but this time he and the pilot walked away from it with minor injuries.

I was so mad; I wanted to kill both of them.

Mickey only had a few scratches, but the pilot broke her nose. It's a good thing she did, because I would probably have done it for her. He didn't get hurt physically, but he got a tongue-lashing from me. Did he fly after that? Oh, yes! And of course at times I had to go with him.

We sometimes flew in late at night. We'd buzz the camp, and somebody would come down and shine their car lights on the runway for us to land.

Another time we were flying down to Palm Beach to meet somebody for dinner. We took off just at dusk and got right over Pratt Whitney Road, and Mickey checked the oil pressure. Zero. He turned around, came back, and just barely got on the strip when the motor stopped. The annual checkup on the plane had just been done, and a screw didn't get tightened back. Nearly all the oil had leaked out.

Mr. Gordon Sparks

Mickey: All this flying around was done in a planes donated to the Camp by our dear friends Gordon and Lucille Sparks. Gordon came to be like an adopted father to me. He had lost a son and I had lost my Dad. He filled that role for me for many years. I just lost him recently and miss him terribly.

He provided planes over the years to assist us in the prison ministry and layman outreach. I'd crash one and he'd simply buy another. (Maybe he should have got a refund back on that flight instructor he hired to give me lessons for my pilot license.) We'd fly in the evenings after I got off work. We didn't have any lights at our little "airport" to guide us in, so when we came in after dark, we would "buzz" the Camp and Laura Maye would drive the truck out and shine the headlights onto the airstrip so we could land. Apparently, I got better at landing in the dark than during the day.

Laura Maye: We lived in those two cottages connected by the added-on room, with tarpaper over the whole thing for years. When we hired B.G. Brown to work with us, Mickey went and had a brand new house built for their family. I was mad. Here I was, living in a tarpaper shack for years, and he builds this guy who just got here a new house! But I got over it. I always got over it, and of course, B.G. and Diane became dear friends and still are to this day. I didn't take things lying down though.

The arrival of Brother B. G. Brown and family to the Camp on July 7th was a real blessing to our ministry.

For a long time it was so wet out here, we had to park the car up on the road. When we got ready to go to leave, we to waded out to the car, carrying our shoes. I took a towel for all of us to dry our feet before we put on shoes and got in the car.

The primitive living conditions were not the only problems I had. I expected Mickey to be like my dad - kind and attentive.   My father had a balanced life with work, family, hunting, and fishing. Mickey never had time for that. He worked eighteen hours a day and came in tired and grouchy. He expected me and the kids to work at the same pace he did. Even before he entered the pastorate, he was always driven.

When we had been here about six years, I got fed up. The Camp was thriving, but out family life was dying. Mickey was working us all to death. We happened to have a missionary friend here, and he could see that something was wrong. He asked me, and I told him, "I'm just sick of this. We don't have any family life. We don't have a decent home. Mickey works day and night." He talked to Mickey, and recommended we go out to the School of Christian Counselors, Narramore Christian Foundation in Rosemead, California. And we did - for a whole month.

The purpose of this seminar was threefold: to help each participant counsel more effectively, to give each of us information regarding professional referrals and to enable each participant to gain a better understanding of himself. Topics covered included personality disturbances, alcoholism, defense mechanisms, character disorders, physiological factors, sex deviation, drug addiction, the nature of childhood, adolescence, the Bible in counseling, pre-marriage counseling and professional techniques of counseling. Mickey told everybody we were going to learn how to counsel, which of course we did, but we also learned a lot about ourselves and each other. We were put through the mill - extensive self-analysis and training on how to deal with our differences.

I learned how bad Mickey's traumatic childhood had emotionally damaged him, and had certainly not equipped him in any way to be a husband or father. He had no idea how to be either. "You need to realize where Mickey is coming from and be the strong one emotionally to mend this marriage," they told me.

The counseling in California changed my whole life.

It made me realize Mickey wasn't trying to ignore me or hurt me. He just wasn't raised like I was, and had no role models. I stopped getting upset and angry over everything. I stopped expecting certain things of him and trying to change him. It made life easier for both of us.

We also realized that a rehabilitation center couldn't succeed working only with the men. The whole family suffers and needs help. If you don't treat the whole family. When we didn't address the issues with the rest of the alcoholic's family, we were missing something important. Even if the man stayed sober, the survival of the family unit was still at risk because the woundedness remained. So we learned a lot just by working through the dysfunction of our own family, which at times was probably worse than the families we were trying to minister *to*. We had to continually work on removing the "planks" out of our own eyes, before we could help others in removing the "splinters" out of theirs.

When we returned from California, we began teaching marriage classes with the men and their wives on weekends. We had learned how to fight constructively, and we taught them - not to turn away from each other but to communicate, try to understand and compromise.

THE EVANS FAMILY

I also came to understand that I didn't have to keep up with Mickey. Just because God told him to do something, did not mean I had to do it too. That freed me up to live my own life - to be a wife and mother and handle the things I felt called to do.

In fact, the only way I have survived at Dunklin all these years was by doing just that – walking my own walk with the Lord's strength, and not trying to walk Mickey's. That, plus the fact that the Lord has provided me with so many wonderful friends over the years.

Friends who have stood in the trenches with us through many hard times and celebrated with us during the good times.

Friends like Theresa Douglas, who I called one afternoon in a panic and said "You've got to help me, Mickey's got all these preachers coming out here tonight, and all I've got to feed them is five pounds of gizzards!

Dunklin's own "Roy Rodgers & Dale Evans"

Theresa and her daughter, Robin

It's a good friend who would answer that call by cooking up a big pan of homemade biscuits 'n gravy and tote it all out to the middle of the woods, then clean and fry five pounds of chicken gizzards! That was one bunch of hungry preachers. (When are preachers not hungry?) I haven't met too many whose belts didn't look like the fence around a fried chicken graveyard. They finished that supper off down to the last gizzard and were glad to get it.

Another friend named Theresa, whose husband was also named Harold, blessed us immensely by taking us along with them on several of their vacations that we would have never been able to afford on our own. One time she even flew with us all the way down to Australia to visit Lauralee where she was working at the time.

Theresa and Harold Campbell

Doris Thorne, Sharon Bell and Dottie Conant lived at the Camp at different times and helped with everything from the cooking to taking care of our kids.

Doris Thorne Bernardi

Later we had angels like Elsie Janagap, Carol Bluman, and Lawrence and Nancy Rhoden who were live in caregivers for our parents.

Charlie and Elsie (Janagap) Nelson

Faye, Mickey and Sandy

Ken and Linda Helser have come down each year from North Carolina to minister.

Jack and Faye Williamson (Haverlant) were some of our dearest friends growing up and raising our families together. Their four girls :Sandy, Linda Faye, Becky and Jennifer are all the same ages as our four children even when the last ones came 14 years after we both thought we were done!

100

Janice and Dr. James Forbes of Clewiston served on our board and hosted home churches and treated the men.

Dr. Sudhir and Manju Nayer came to the States in the early 70's. They have worked tirelessly since then to provide financial support of their free hospital back in India. They, and their son Guatam, have been dear friends for many years. They have treated men in the program, made countless housecalls, helped us with our growing list of aches and pains, volunteered their medical expertise and emotional support time and time again, and have become part of our family.

Dr. Sudhir and Manju Nayer

Wayne and Doris Cole, Jamie and Jackie Buckingham ,

Bob and Betty Moody

Emory and Onnie Jean Walker, Bud and Beth Gubler, John and Theresa Roberts, Gary and Gwen Marsh,

Johnnie and Peter Lord

Bill and Betty Clemons, Timer and Kettie Powers, Norman and Carol Hales, Tiny and Vivian Durrance, Dan and Irene Jones, Homer and Iris Wall, Jerry and Jaunita Walker , George and Gloria Diaz, Bill and

Nancy and Jerry Jolicoeur

Mary Cheshire, Ron and Janis Ross , Bill and Betty Clemons, Rose and Jim Shoptaw, W.A. and Nancy Howell...the list is too long and my memory is too short, but they and many

Donna and Guy Strayhorn

others have all been such an important part of our Dunklin Family.

w/ Damon and Betty Walker, Betty and Sonny W illiamson

Many of them have already gone on to Heaven, and we look forward to having a "family reunion" with them soon.

Dr. Roger and Miriam Hatton

And of course, there I are Gene and Nell, who have been our friends and neighbors and also helped at the Camp in numerous ways. Nell has been like a sister to me for the last thirty years. I don't know what I'd have done without her. She has such a servant's heart and is always willing to help me with anything. She's been like the hands and feet of Jesus to me over the years. We've had so many fun times. Sometimes all we do is just look at each other and laugh over all our blunders as we are getting old and at all the adventure we had when we were younger. We've had our share of differences as well – especially when it comes to politics! But we've learned to just laugh about it and go on having fun. Nowadays the most trouble we get into is trying to beat Liz at playing cards!

Back to Mickey: "Al and I had been "batching" it at the Camp, while we hand-cleared the jungle to start the buildings. Plans weren't to open the ministry until summer. I was actually

Mickey and Al Cross

away in Missouri preaching a revival, when the first man showed up at the Camp looking for help. His need was urgent, so Al and Laura Maye took him in. Another man soon followed the first, then another and another. By the time I got back, ready or not, the operation was in full swing. So the ministry was prematurely born ahead of

Mickey Evans Revivalist At Tropical Farms Chapel

Mickey Evans, pastor of Dunklin Memorial Baptist Church at Indiantown, and one of the outstanding young preachers of the area, will begin a series of revival services Sunday night at Tropical Farms Baptist Chapel, six miles south of Stuart. These services will continue through the week, beginning each evening at 7:30.

Pastor Evans was born in Okeechobee and grew up in that community with a love for cattle and ranch work. Though later entering the ministry, he still enjoys saddling up and riding with cowboy friends and, while making pastoral calls, if he chances on a cattle drive he is apt to join in, should a spare horse be handy.

Mickey received his preparation for the ministry at Carson-Newman College in Tennessee and at New Orleans Baptist Seminary. Before as pastor to Indiantown he taught school for a

our timetable, but right on God's schedule.

We found four small tourist cottages for sale in Ft. Pierce. A company wanted them moved to make room for a modern motel. I borrowed $2000 from Faye's daddy, John Abney. He said, "Pay me back when you can, Mickey." We moved them to the property, placed two of them side-by-side on crossties, built a room in between to connect them and in November of 1963, my family took up full-time residence at the Camp.

Our Camp family was tiny at first. Al Cross, Ma and Pa Campbell, Tom and Lilly Nix and my own family were the first staff. We had few tools to work with, and little idea what running an alcoholic rehabilitation center was all about. It was exciting but frustrating. What do you do with thirty sober and sobering alcoholics? We learned together. The men learned about the Lord, and we learned about alcoholism.

We had the two extra cottages to house Al and the men who would come to us for help.   I bought a big tent from a Pentecostal evangelist, Bro. Thigpen, from Ortona on the East side of Lake Okeechobee. He had fallen on good times and was able to purchase a new one. The leaky tent served as our first tabernacle, and we held our first Campmeeting in it December 26, 1963.

"Camp Meeting 20 miles"

Pa Campbell feeding orphaned pet fawn

After the first Campmeeting, we began having services in the tent on Friday nights. The mosquitoes were so bad we didn't pass the offering can – We passed the can of OFF. We would back up a truck to the entrance with a fogger in the bed and "smoke" the tent to push them back for a little while. One night the pet deer ran right up into the middle of the meeting, trying to escape the suckers.

If it rained hard, water would run through the floor of the tent. Boardwalks would have to be put down so the ladies didn't bog down walking through the tent.

But in spite of the mosquitoes and mud, we had some truly glorious times under that old tent. It felt like we were touching Heaven when folks gathered there from all sorts of different denominations to worship and praise the Lord in one accord. Every Friday night it would be filled to capacity and the sides f would reverberate with the sounds of rejoicing. We experienced firsthand the glory of the Lord, as it swept over us time and time again.

Folks came from far and wide, for the sweet fellowship and fantastic fish-fries.

We went through three tents over the years. We kept the first tent up for 3-4 years. Then we loaned it out to several groups to start new churches. Shiloh Youth Ranch, Salerno Baptist Church, Hobe Sound Baptist Church and Trinity Temple were all "birthed" out of that first old tent.

Norman Peterson, Bob Crowe, Mickey, Tedd Lott, Sonny Holland, Henry Tatum, Adrian Rodgers

Outstanding pastors came to preach: Adrian Rogers, Peter Lord, Ted Lott, Damon Walker and Tiny Durrance. One night Tiny preached "What do you do with your blind calves, your cull oranges and your cooter-tail cucumbers?" He - could really "shell-the-corn" (meaning relate to country people). I thought the sermon was so good, I made it the cover of our next

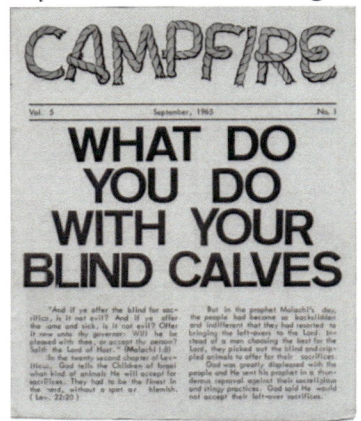

month's Campfire.

One time Tiny- who was anything but- came to the camp to preach on Ephesians 5: 15 "See *then that you walk circumspectly, not as fools but as wise redeeming the time, because the days are evil."*

Tiny said he had just that day, learned the meaning of walking circumspectly. He had been out quail hunting that morning, and almost stepped on a rattlesnake.
He said "The rest of the day I was walking circumspectly, looking all around for evil."

That was both a good spiritual and practical lesson for us. Huge ground rattlers and water moccasins were abundant in these piney woods and swamps back then. We killed several well over six feet long. I believe it was only by the Lord's protection that no one died from snakebite while we were clearing the land.

Rev. Tiny Durrance

1Laura Maye feeding much friendlier wildlife

One of the families I met while in Cuba sent their son, to Florida to work on Lykes Ranch to learn English. His father was a foreman for Lykes in Cuba. He was good on equipment and would come up to visit help us clear land when he got time off. We had kind of adopted him.

Laura Maye, Clint (in the operator's seat) with Adan Gibson, David, Dean and Ma Campbell

When Adan got ready to go back home, I accompanied him. Just as we were getting ready to board the plane in Miami, I noticed some buzzards circling the airport and pointed them out to Adan. I was joking when I told him that was a bad sign for our flight, but he wasn't joking when he turned back to me and said " I'll see you back in Cuba, Preacher – I'm takin the boat!"

Cooking coffee on a bedframe

"It's far better to build a boy, than mend a man". Camp meetings, youth camps and retreats were part of the foundation upon which the Camp was built.

Softball swingers

One summer Jamie Buckingham led a summer camp to train young people to live and minister on Kibbutz communities in Israel. We really enjoyed having them here. The instructors welcomed us to join in learning about the Jewish culture and even taught us some Hebrew and dances. It was wonderful worshipping the Lord in His "native tongue" as we danced and sang together.

Jamie had taken me with him through the Sinai desert twice and he had a real heart for the Holy Land and took seriously the biblical admonition to
"Pray for the peace of Jerusalem." He had witnessed firsthand the violence inflicted on the Israeli people by the radical arm of the P.L.O. Once, I was with him as he took a team of the Kibbutz kids to help clean up a town in Lebanon after a period of fierce fighting. Many of the buildings had been bombed out and the dead were everywhere. We came upon a church where a group of

men, women and children had been lined up along the outside wall and shot to death in cold blood. As Jamie helped me inside through a shattered window a shard of glass severed a vein in my leg and my own blood joined with theirs.

At the moment it happened, I cidn't even feel or notice it because I was aghast at what I saw inside. It had been a Catholic church and the Crucifix had been riddle by machine guns, until only the arms of Christ were left hanging. Finally, they had desecrated the altar with excrement.

Altogether, it was a horrific scene that remains burned in my mind. May we all continue to lift up Jamie's prayer daily for the peace of Jerusalem.

Jamie Buckingham

Chapter 10:
Constructing a City in the Wilderness

We accepted any kind of help people offered us, and we had a steady supply of willing laborers among the

recovering alcoholics who came for help. They took pride in helping build the camp, and we felt it belonged to each of them.

For a time, we had men living in old school buses and tent-camper trailers. We had nowhere else to house them, but they didn't complain, they were just grateful to be a part of what the Lord was doing, and they way He had changed their lives.

"DMC Rolling Overflow Dorm"

Tom and Lillie Nix left a beautiful home in Okeechobee, and moved to the Camp into one of other the little fishing cottages, the one by where we still baptize. Tom, who gave up a successful career as a building contractor, oversaw all of our early construction and was a general all around good hand.

Lily and Tom Nix

EARL WILLIAMS TROWELING

THE BLESSING OF THE BAR

There was a little country bar and package store in Indiantown where everybody knew your name. The bartender was a congenial guy, and the regular crowd enjoyed a social bonding of mutual acceptance. The drinks served at the bar stimulated physical relaxation and sociability. Only occasionally would a social drinker slip across the invisible line to become a dependent drinker causing him to exhibit antisocial and sometimes even hostile behavior.

For instance, the time a deputy sheriff's ear got bit off, when he attempted to interrupt a friendly fight between two cowboys who swore allegiances to different football teams. Neither had graduated from high school, but they were loyal Gator and Seminole fans. Besides that, what right did a deputy have, interfering when these good ole boys got a little physical in the Happy Hour?

Unfortunately, the elixir that produces positive feelings of euphoria and sociability has a side effect called addiction, and one out of ten social drinkers become alcoholics. They can control when they start drinking but not when they stop. Their social drinking deteriorates to antisocial behavior that causes them to make drinking a priority over their families and jobs. It also radically changes their value systems. We found the bill of sale for a man's whole house full of furniture that he had given up to pay his bar tab lying on the floor when we started cleaning it up.

The little wooden bar had a lot of stories to tell. It had left its mark on the community of Indiantown. Fortunately for the bartender, business had been so profitable that the owner decided to replace the little store with a larger concrete block structure that could hold more people. The little bar was a historical monument in Indiantown, but business is business, and a house mover was hired to haul the building away.

I was shocked when my friend, Clayton White, the house-mover, called to ask if I would like to have the old bar at Dunklin. My first thought was "What will my friends think if I, a Baptist preacher, bought a bar?" My mind went into overdrive as I began imagining the gossip that the Indiantown bar would create sitting in the center of an alcohol and drug recovery camp.

Naturally, we made it an immediate object of prayer. Two things motivated our prayers. First, did God want to put converted drunks in the same building that had contributed to their problem? Second, if He did, where would we get the $300 to pay for it?

Al Cross and I knelt on the ground and poured out our situation to God. In a little while, Al stopped praying and smiled at me. He said, "Mickey, I have been drunk in that old building many times. If God can convert me, He can convert a bar too!"

At that point, we were holding our classes in the tent, and cooking outdoors on the open grill made out of a box spring. Anything was an improvement over that. So, it was settled. We wanted the Indiantown Bar, but where would we get the $300?

We prayed again, and the Lord said, "You've already got the money." I said, "Where is it, Lord?" He reminded me that Sonny had recently offered to donate the bond he bought when we were raising money for the new church building in Indiantown. I just hadn't had a chance to get out to his place to pick it up.

We didn't even have the radio out there yet, so I drove to Sonny's ranch, north of Okeechobee, and asked if he still wanted to give the bond to us. He said, "Sure. It's in the drawer." I asked him how much it was for, and he told me $250. "But, it has some interest coupons on it too." When he added them up it came to "$50." That is how we bought the bar.

The moving of the bar to our wilderness camp was an event that required only two days of hard work, but we had a lot of cleaning to do. We discovered the names of some of my former church members on IOU tabs left in the drawers under the counter. The building smelled like a bar. Al commented, "Funny I never noticed the smell when I was drinking in here."

Within two weeks, a group of ex-drunks converted the old building from a bar to a kitchen, dining room, classroom and church. Ex-addicts and their families gathered on Sundays to worship the Lord, and to thank Him for their deliverance from alcoholism.

"Oh, what joy for those whose disobedience
is forgiven, ...whose sin is no longer counted
against them by the Lord."
Romans 4:7,8

After that, I guess word got out, and if a building was scheduled to be demolished anywhere nearby, the owner called us to tear it down and haul the material out to the Camp. We salvaged and recycled the lumber from Adrian Rogers' church and several houses in Ft. Pierce.

THE FIRST DORM

The salvaged lumber from Susie McGlaughlin's Boarding House and the old First Baptist Church of Okeechobee building where Brother Mickey was ordained, made up the materials for this, the first dormitory which housed seven men. After construction of the larger dorms, it was converted into the "Haberdashery," a place to organize and store clothing and other items donated toward meeting the needs of the men, many of which arrived with nothing but the clothes they had on. The Haberdashery ministry is a labor of love carried out by Miss Mary, Martha and Margaret Hulen.

THE TOMATOE HOUSE

The little cabin that served as our first office was a migrant labor house in Ft. Pierce. Got knocked off its blocks by a tomato truck, owner of the labor camp called and offered it to us, we hired Jim Tucker to move it to the Camp, it was later refurbished by our son, Dean into the camp clinic.

GUIDED BY GENEROSITY

We have also been blessed by business men and community leaders like Timer Powers and C.J. King who were propane gas business owners who rounded up their colleagues and not only donated but also laid themselves all the gas lines through the Camp in one day. These men and many like them exemplified the generosity of Jesus and walked out their faith.

While preaching a revival at the Baptist Church in Okeechobee, a dentist -Dr. Carl Arant, came up to me afterward and offered to serve on our Board of Directors.

A few days later he showed up at the camp with a friend, Freeman Hales who owned Home Milk Co. Dairies down in Miami. Freeman was the father of Norman Hales who had given me the $3000 earnest money to purchase the land.

They walked around looking at the Camp. It didn't take long, because there wasn't much to see at that time. We had refurbished the old bar and schoolhouse where we held classes and ate meals, and built a Fellowship Hall from salvaged lumber where we held the Saturday night sings and church on Sundays. As we walked, I told them my hopes and dreams for dormitories and a tabernacle to worship in. When they got ready to leave Mr. Hales pulled out a check, stuck it in my pocket and said, "Here's a little something to help you with your building program." I was kind of bashful about pulling it out in front of him, so I thanked him, and they left. When I pulled out the check it was for $50,000! In 1965, $50,000 went a long way. With this generous gift, we were able to build an air conditioned Tabernacle, a dormitory, another staff house, and also a small canning plant

We were seeing Jehovah-Jireh, "the God who provides" work miracle after miracle as He put His "City of Refuge" together piece by piece. It was amazing to see how He placed people with specific skills here at just the right time.

"Kairos" is a Greek term meaning "God's specially appointed time". Just one example of this "kairos" timing we witnessed was when the Tabernacle was erected. We got a great price on a steel structure "kit" . We bought it from a company in Leesburg who had custom fabricated it for a client who defaulted on payment. The catch was the blueprints belonged to the customer, so the kit was sold "as is" with no directions for constructing it. When the pieces were delivered we had no idea how to begin putting it together. I went into the chowhall where the men were gathered for class and asked if any of them had any experience in construction. I just about fell over when five of the men immediately raised their hands and each said they had been *steel workers* at one time or another. Now understand, there were only about twelve men total in the program at that time. Those five men and a crane operator set the steel for the Tabernacle's framework in *one day*!

THE SCHOOLHOUSE THAT BECAME A CHURCH HOUSE

We purchased the old Hobe Sound Schoolhouse for $50 and moved it out to the Camp. Theresa and Harold Campbell converted the side rooms for the men to do ceramics to give their wives and children complete with a kiln in the back room. Phyllis Sehon carried on this ministry until it was discontinued when she fell ill. Now its the Canteen and "Rec" Hall - in the past, it also housed a one chaired barbershop and weightlifting room.

Schoolhouse converted to a Church, Chow Hall, Classroom

"Man shall not live by bread alone, but by every word that proceedeth out of the mouth of God" Matthew 4:4

As we outgrew the schoolhouse our first
TABERNACLE FELLOWSHIP / DINING HALL
was constructed.

Delivering Cement The Hard Way

Faye Williamson and Laura Maye at pianos

Singing in the open aired tabernacle with straw floor
took on a higher note when the chairs would tip over
and start a chain reaction down the rows.
Miss Mildred Lindsey (on front row left) helped with the revivals.

123

"GUEST" DORM

Originally built for guests and used for Emmaus Walk weekends, the "Guest Dorm" also served as Sunday School Rooms. As the program grew, the guest dorm turned into full time dormitory housing for men in the program.

Dale and Ida Baugh

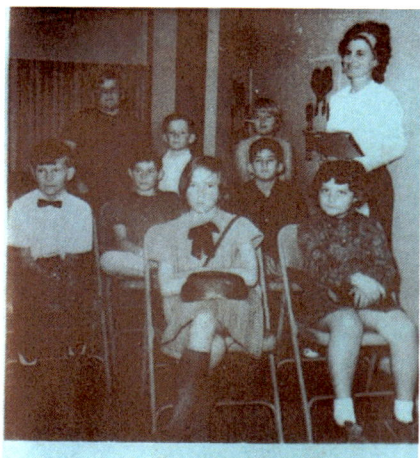

Doris Swearington & Class

Doris Swaringen was the first Sunday School Teacher at Dunklin. She loved children and taught children to love the Lord.
Her legacy was then carried on by Ida and Dale Baugh who were faithful to love countless kids into the Kingdom.
Mrs. Pamela Barber now carries their torch lighting the path for the next generation to cherish His Word as "lamp unto their feet".

GOOD SAMARITAN INN

In The "Good Sam" as it is known, was built in 1979. More rooms were needed for the men's families to visit on the weekends. A design was incorporated that featured a large meeting area surrounded by motel style bedrooms wrapped around the perimeter. The project was paid for by Mr. Bill Lecki, a recovering alcoholic who owned a coal mine in West Virginia. Gene and Mike Williams poured the concrete, Emory Walker donated all 25 air conditioners and the Park Avenue Baptist Church pastored by Peter Lord in Titusville donated video studio equipment to record teachings for distribution to prisons and other rehabilitation facilities.

The men in the program look forward to spending weekends with their families in Dunklin's own "Holy-day Inn"

Where Lake Elijah is now, was all low sand-pond, full of water in rainy season, and dry the rest of the year. Where the sawmill is, was a snake and gator-infested swamp. Harold Douglas who was an expert dragline operator brought his machine and his expertise in running it. He is the reason we have Prayer Island today.

Allapattah Ranch also provided heavy equipment to dig ponds and clear palmettos. Their mechanic would also work on our equipment. He was the only person who could crank the bulldozer so every time we used it he would have to come and get it started.

CAMP BLESSINGS

Sonny loaned us their D-4 bulldozer to clear the land along with his foreman, Hubert Waldron, to operate it. This picture is of a TD-18 dozier donated by Mr. Jimmy Davis of the Davis Meadowbrook Dairy in Ft. Pierce.

Numerous others donated supplies, equipment and expertise to help the Camp get started, and many of those same people who were there for the beginning have remained so faithful, continuing their support for all these years.

Lynn Beville and Reece Hataway work on the airstrip.

LAOS TRAINING CENTER

Outreach and Ministry Training have always been hallmark goals in Dunklin's mission. We often say, "We are not a "drying out place" for drug addicts and alcoholics, we are a training center for Christian soldiers".

Reid Harden was the director of the Renewal Evangelism program of the Southern Baptist Convention Home Mission Board, and founder of Layman's Landing Ministries. In 1972, he and I put our dreams of a lay training center together and started Laos Institute. Laos means "People of God" in the Greek language. Reid and his wife Phyllis, dreamed of training laymen to renew the institutional church. I dreamed of training recovering alcoholics to reach other active alcoholics and to invade Florida prisons with the Gospel. The same message fit both needs, so we bought back forty acres of land adjoining the Camp for the training center.

Reid Hardin

LAOS OPENING

Board of Directors

I will never forget the prayer meeting we held concerning purchasing the property. Thirty men prayed through the night and God gave us a powerful go-ahead sign as he poured out His Spirit on us.

That same week, Garland Eastham, founder of Faith Farms, another Christ centered rehab program, drove up to the Camp to tell me that God had spoken to him to tell me to start the training center, and he loaned us the money to buy the land.

David Sparks

On the forty acres that we purchased adjacent to DMC we built a six-bedroom lodge that provides facilities for small groups. It was repaid two months later by Gordon and Lucille Sparks as a memorial to their son, David, who had completed our program and later died in a tragic accident.

Additional property on the east side of the Camp that had been a piece of the original tract but was sold to cover the mortgage was later repurchased from Raymond and Lillian Drum who were also a part of the Camp family and volunteered here until their health failed. The parcel came to be known as "Gethsemane" for its peace and solitude.

The original Laos retreat center, now our main offices with the Laos Lodge addition on the original's left side.

BRO. J. B.
WOODHAM,
FROM
OKEECHOBEE

Arlund
Woodham

Chapter: 11
Hard Lessons Learned

Mickey: In the very early days of Dunklin, before we learned how dangerous it could be for them and us, we would take men in right off the streets and allow them to detox here. We dubbed one of the little cabins next to ours "the drunk tank". Sometimes - and I don't know what we were thinking - but since Dean was already interested in medicine at fourteen- and if there was no one else who could be there at the time, we would actually put him in there to monitor and help the men as they endured the horrible vomiting, hallucinations and seizures that are brought on by withdrawal.

Luckily, it had been Al who had been sitting up with this one man, who was having severe D.T.'s On the fourth night he seemed to be getting a little better, so I told Al to go on back to his room in the dorm and get some rest. I would get up and checked on him through the night. All of the sudden I heard this loud banging and ran over there to find him just going crazy and tearing up the place. I was able to eventually get him calmed down and back to bed, but thought I'd better just spend the rest of the night on the other bunk next to him.

I had just drifted back off to sleep when I was jolted awake to find him standing over me with a knife that looked as big as a machete in that moment. I could tell by the crazed look in his eyes that he was in the middle of a hallucination, and apparently thought I was the Boogie man come to get him. I didn't know what to do. He was between me and the only way out.

I was afraid to make a move. I stood there and said a silent prayer asking the Lord how to handle this situation.

I didn't want either one of us to get hurt, but I wasn't seeing a way around it. Then it was like something just came over him and I could see the change in his eyes. I quietly asked him for the knife and held out my hand...and just as calmly he handed it over.

After that episode, Laura Maye laid down the law and declared no more detoxing next to her house. So from then on we took men to the hospital in Okeechobee where my cousin H.H. Raulerson and two other doctors, Dr. Horton and Dr. Beech volunteered their services to help the men, on the condition that one of us remain there with them to keep them from hurting any other patients. We still had to pay the hospital though, and after a while we ran up such a bill that they decided since we didn't have the money, we could pay them back by bringing in the men to paint the whole hospital. This was certainly a fair trade, since our men had been responsible for bangin up a lot of the walls in the first place!

AFTERCARE

Soon we started to realize that not only did these men need specialized help before they came in to the program, by way of detox, but that they also need help and support after they left the program to make the transition into a lifestyle of sobriety.

We set out to provide this by way of establishing what we called "Good Samaritan Fellowship Clubs." Which spread throughout the state of Florida. These were the pre-cursers to what are now known as "Overcomer Groups".

> *"We ask God to give you a complete understanding of what He wants to do in your lives, and we ask Him to make you wise with spiritual wisdom. Then the way you live will always honor and please the Lord, and you will continually do good, kind things for others.*
>
> *All the while, you will learn to know God better and better. We also pray that you will be strengthened with His glorious power so that you will have all the patience and endurance you need.*
>
> *May you be filled with joy, always thanking the Father, who has enabled you to share the inheritance that belongs to God's holy people, who live in the light.*
>
> *For He has rescued us from the one who rules in the in the kingdom of darkness, and He has brought us into the Kingdom of His dear Son. God has purchased our freedom with His blood and has forgiven all our sins."*
> *Colossians 1:9-14*

Charter Group of the Good Samaritan Fellowship Clubs

Rev. Will Teasley and his wife came on board to oversee this Aftercare arm of the ministry, and established our first half-way house called the "Good Samaritan Home" in Fort Pierce in 1968. With none other than Oliver "Red" Fox being one of the first house managers.

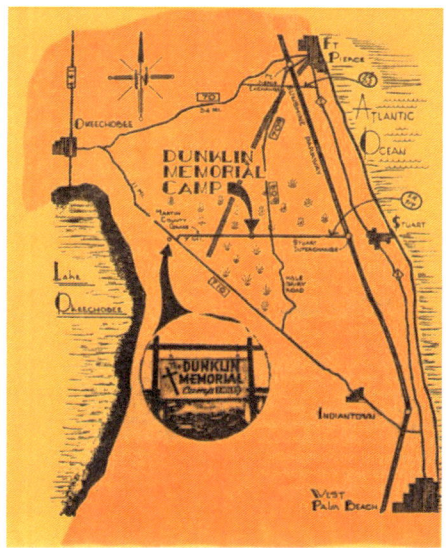

TAKING RESPONSIBILITY

His name was Earle Raiford. I knew him well, had grown up right across the road from him. He came into the program. One day we found out that he was getting high on prescription medication the doctor had given him for an injury. We told him he had to give them up. He said he couldn't do that, so we dismissed him.

He went to town, got a room ... got some whisky, and drank himself to death. He was in that room three days before somebody found him.

When that happened, I almost ...no, I did ... have a nervous breakdown. Between being burned out from overwork, and feeling guilty about Earl's death, the Devil camped on me and said, "If you hadn't dismissed him he would be alive today. It's your fault he's dead." I believed the lie, took it to heart, and it wiped me out.

I was paralyzed by the guilt and fear that it would happen again if I made the wrong decision about a man. It got to where I could not make a decision of any kind. We had good people on our Board of Directors, and some of them recognized that I needed to get away. So they sent Laura Maye and I off for a whole month to Hot Springs, Arkansas. We soaked in those springs and had a good long rest. During that time, the Lord taught me a powerful lesson.

Whenever a man falls or dies from an overdose - if we take responsibility for it, we are unconsciously taking responsibility for the successes, too. We take credit for it. "Look here, I did a good job." This man is making it. If the man falls, conversely we think, "I did a bad job."When you take responsibility of other people's behavior, that is co-dependency, and it will destroy you. When you're in this kind of work, it will kill you.

I learned it is not our decision either way. If a man makes it, it is because God helped him. If he fails it's because he did not do what God told him to do. It's not about us. It's about the man and his relationship with God. If a man doesn't learn that early in his ministry, he'll never last long in recovery. Because there are a lot of relapses. If we take responsibility for everyone who relapses, it will kill us. If you're not careful you over-balance the other way and you get hard. Your heart will get hard, and you don't really care about the men. There has to be a balance. It's learning that this is God's program, and it's a man's relationship with God and not the program, or the people who run the program that counts.

> "We pray to God that you will not do anything wrong.
> We pray this, not to show that our ministry to you
> has been successful, but because we want you to
> do right even if we ourselves seem to have failed.
> Our responsibility is never to oppose the truth,
> but to stand for truth at all times.
> We are glad to be weak, if you are really strong.
> What we pray for is your restoration
> to maturity."
> II Corinthians 13:7-9

IT ALL COMES CRASHING DOWN

The plane crash...actually, there was more than one.. But one of them taught me a valuable lesson about running a one-man show.

Laura Maye and I used to fly often to meetings around the state. I flew for thirty years, over 3,000 hours, but all Laura Maye likes to tell about are the accidents.

She didn't like to land at night out here on this grassy runway. As we would roll safely to a stop on the ground, I would say, "Honey, we've cheated death again." She didn't think that was funny. One night a flock of sheep broke through the fence and ran out on the runway just as I was taxiing in. I couldn't avoid them and the plane flipped upside-down. We ate mutton for months!

But the lesson I learned about trying to run everything myself came in 1975. After preaching at the Sunday morning service at Dunklin, I climbed into the four-passenger, 172 Cessna, and took off alone from the landing strip at the Camp and headed for my aunt's ranch in Venus, Florida. One of my cousins had been killed in an auto accident, and I was sent to break the tragic news to his grandmother. By this time, I had been flying fifteen years and was used to making quick trips around the state. As I was making my approach, a hard rain started to set in, and I could not see the power lines as I banked the Cessna to land on the paved road near the ranch. In a split second, I saw them and tried to duck under. It was too late.

I nosed into the ground. Watching in horror as the plane crashed, were my mother and several cousins. They rushed to the wreckage, pulled me out and laid me on the roadway until an ambulance arrived to transport me to a hospital in Sebring twenty miles away.

My back was broken. I couldn't walk, couldn't even move. In the hospital, I was a week or two on drugs around the clock. I was given enough Morphine to put down a horse. So much that it actually stopped my heart. After that, they took me off it - just like that -cold turkey. My back went into spasms. If anyone touched the bed, my back would immediately break into spasms, causing horrendous pain.

I went 3 days nights without sleep, and on the fourth, I cried out to God in the middle of the night, "Lord, let me die and get out of this pain. I can't stand it any longer!" Then I said something stupid. "Lord why are you doing this to me?" I was crazy with pain, or I wouldn't have asked a question like that. Remembering Job, I immediately regretted it. But at that moment, when my faith reached its lowest point, Jesus walked in the room at Sebring Hospital.

I felt His presence and knew He was there. He said, "Mickey, I wasn't flying that plane. You were."

My mind immediately cleared, I felt His presence all over me, and I thought, "He's come to heal me. He's going to say the word, and I'm going to jump up out of this bed, walk out of the hospital and go back to work."

But He didn't. That was all He said to me, but His presence did not leave. I felt at peace and finally went to sleep.

A few days later they got me up using a walker. I could only manage five steps or so, but it was a beginning. When I was able to leave the hospital they didn't want us to go far. A good buddy of ours from Pahokee, Frank Tillis, had a cousin named Mel (yep, that one) who offered to let us stay at his lake house there in Sebring. Each day I used the walker to get down to the lake, and exercise my legs in the water.

Back at the Camp, the reaction to the crash had been immediate. The whole ministry almost came crashing down with the plane. For almost twelve years, I had been running a one-man-show, and that is like building a house on sand. The Lord was about to teach me another hard lesson, the hard way...the only way I seemed to lean them.

Everyone had been working under me and had no authority over any part of the ministry. I hadn't taken the time to train anyone. That was a big mistake.

Nobody had been prepared, but everyone tried to take over running the Camp. When we realized the ministry was real danger of collapsing, we decided to completely shut it down until we could sort things out. Some of the men stayed on because they didn't have anywhere to go, but we just shut the work down until we could fix the problems. Several people were fired, and we began changing our governmental system.

We split up the workload and responsibilities, regrouped and began again. After three months, I was able to get back to work - wearing a brace – but like my back, my pride had been broken, and I was humbled

enough to accept help and delegate responsibilities.

Jean, Gracie and Monty King were a great help on the staff at this time.

Gary and Janis Dickinson were also a special blessing.

THE DICKINSONS

At the same time, we were learning that the problem is finding people who are trained and healthy enough themselves to help others. If people are not trained in this ministry, they sometimes want to help out of their own co-dependence. They haven't dealt with their own problems, and may just need to be needed. They often show up with more problems than the people they are trying to help.

FUNDRAISING

The Lord taught me a very humbling lesson one year about faith and finances. The only annual fundraiser we have ever promoted is our "Yearling a Year" Love Offering. This is when we ask our local ranchers to earmark the sale of a calf at the Livestock Market to be donated to Dunklin. The idea came from the Lord, and He has blessed this offering over the years and multiplied it.

Well, one year I learned an lesson like Father Abraham did. Abraham decided to "take matters into his own hands" and help God along with providing him an heir. The child "Ishmael" born from his slavewoman became a thorn in his side. The child born by a miracle God did through his wife was the true heir to the blessing.

So, one year things were looking lean and I let this slick "Christian" fund raising adviser talk me into sending out a mass mailing asking for money. The money poured in, but the conviction came with it that the Lord was not pleased with our "fleshly" efforts. He Lord made me send back every penny of the money that came in from that mailing, along with a letter of apology. It may be fine for other ministries, but the Lord made it very clear that was not the way He wanted to us to raise capital.

Chapter 12:
When the Spirit Moves...

Mickey: Bob Crowe pastored a church down in Miami and was coming up to sing in one of our early Camp revival meetings. Adrian Rogers was talking about him one day and said, "You know Bob's a mystic."

"What's a mystic?" I asked.

"Well, he's a man of prayer. He's been filled with the Spirit - had the Baptism of the Holy Spirit," he said. "And he speaks in tongues."

Laura Maye's mother had received the Baptism and had told me about it, but I had been off to college and was taught that was for another day - not for us now. At that time in the early 1960's very few Baptists believed in the Baptism of the Holy Spirit, and I'd never heard of one who spoke in tongues.   During the revival a few days later, I asked Bob to tell me about his experience. He had sought to be filled with the Spirit for a long time and had finally received.

I said, "I want you to pray for me and teach me about the Baptism." "Okay," he said. "I will if you'll come and preach a revival for me down in Miami."

So I went to Miami.

Bob Crowe at one of the first tent meetings

We began staying up nearly all night praying. Sometimes Bob would pray for me in tongues. I was twisting the Lord's arm saying, "Lord, I've got to have this." Nothing happened. Night after night, we kept praying.

The last night of the revival, we prayed nearly all night, and I was tired. We were visiting in the daytime and preaching every night. I went upstairs in Bob's church alone and sat in his study and said, "Lord, I'm not going to ask you anymore. If this is for me I want it. If not, I'll accept the fact that it's not for me."

There was nobody in the room with me, and it was quiet. I just started speaking in tongues. I felt like a by-stander. I wasn't excited or jumping around. I was just sitting there calm … speaking in tongues.

It changed my prayer life.

Several Baptist Preachers found out about us having the Baptism, and they came to us to pray for them individually. Several were filled, and a couple went back and told their congregations about it and got kicked out of their churches.

The gift of tongues is the Spirit of the Lord inside you praying in an unknown language. It's a prayer language. It's a sacred thing.

The Baptism of the Spirit is simply the filling of the Spirit. The gift of tongues is just one of nine gifts given by the Holy Spirit listed in Corinthians…wisdom, knowledge, faith, healing, miracles, prophecy, discernment, tongues and interpretation of tongues. Many people think tongues are the only evidence of being filled with the Spirit.

Bob Mumford, one of the leaders of the charismatic movement, says fire and persecution are the evidence of being filled. You can expect Satan to attack you whenever you manifest the power of God. Bob is a man speaking from maturity and experience.

Bob and Judith Mumford with their children at the Camp

I majored in Bible at college, attended seminary had never learned about the work of the Holy Spirit. It was in the Bible, but we were not taught about it. Nobody taught much about prayer either.

When I began to study about prayer and the great prayer masters over the years, all were men who were filled with the Spirit. They didn't describe tongues as the evidence. It was an intimacy with the Lord they noted. When I received the Baptism of the Holy Spirit, I felt an intimacy with the Lord I had never felt before.

I believe the Lord was also setting the stage for years later, when He sent a man named Mark Virkler to the Camp who taught me the simple, yet profound art of "prayer journaling". This type of journaling turns prayer into a two way conversation *with God* instead of a monologue to God. This simple revelation - that God still speaks to us personally, just as He has always done in the past, totally revolutionized my life and program at Dunklin. Have you ever considered the fact that most of the text in Bible is just that? – God speaking to people, and them writing down what He said!?

We went from "giving a man a fish" (generally teaching men *about* God) to "teaching a man to fish" (letting God speak for Himself to each man personally) providing daily spiritual sustenance for a lifetime beyond the program.

THE HOLY SPIRIT TRESSPASSES ON THE COUNRTY CLUB

One of the most powerful manifestations of the working of the Holy Spirit that I have witnessed was in a meeting where I ministered with Austin Brown. Aust n and I had met when he was an inmate at Belle Glade prison, serving a 15 year sentence for murder. The Lord redeemed him, filled him with a powerful dose of the Holy Spirit, and placed a strong calling on his life. In a miraculous turn of events, his sentence was reduced to time served, and upon his release, I invited him join us at to Dunklin for ministry training.

The president of General Development, the company who was responsible for building most of the city of Port Saint Lucie, was a member of the First Baptist church of South Miami. He invited the pastor and the deacons from his church up to the Saint Lucie Country Club for a retreat and asked if I would speak to them. So I took Austin with me. I took him to prisons, and almost everywhere I went in those days to give his astonishing testimony.

We got there and I prayed, "Lord what do you want me to tell these people?" I was feeling out-classed by men of First Baptist Church of Miami. The Lord said "Have a foot-washing."

I said, "No, Lord. These people wouldn't understand that at all." Arguing with the Lord doesn': work. It's like spittin' against the wind.

When it came time for me to speak, we were all sitting around this room. I read the thirteenth chapter of John where Jesus washed the disciples' feet: *"If ye know these things, happier are ye if ye do them. If I your master wash your feet then you should wash one another's feet."*

I read that and sat down with a pan of water. I didn't have anything else to say.

We just sat there for what seemed like an hour. Those men stared at me, and then at Austin, back at me, then Austin. This was in an area where black men were not readily accepted - especially in Country Clubs.

Finally, the pastor got up with a strange look on his face that I couldn't quite decipher, and I thought for a moment, Uh-oh. I'm going to get it now.

He came over, got the pan, knelt down before Austin, and washed his feet. He dried them, then stood up and hugged him. He backed away from Austin and said, "Brother, I have to confess. You are the first black man I have ever hugged in my life. And this is the first time I've ever washed anybody's feet, but God told me to do it."

When he said that the Spirit of the Lord fell on those men and they started washing one another's feet and getting right with each other. It was a powerful time, really nothing short of a miracle.

In March of 1975, we ordained Austin in the Tabernacle at Dunklin. He had been hired as a chaplain at Florida State Prison to work with Max Jones. Austin's wedding and ordination was a beautiful example of Christian love bridging the gap between races. The Lord has used Austin and Jeanette to break down many walls of prejudice that once separated the body of Christ. It was a beautiful sight, not only because Jeannette was a beautiful bride, which indeed she was, but it was also a clear picture of how our unity in  Christ erases all lines of race, culture, background or anything else that Satan has used over the ages to divide people.

I always requested that Austin to sing *"I'll Fly Away"* at Homecoming services. Darned if he didn't do just that a few years ago and left me behind. I always knew he would get into Heaven before me!

Janelle, Rosa, Mickey and Jeanette Brown

Jeannette and his four amazing daughters: Jawanda, Austine, Janelle and Rosa are all carrying on his legacy of serving the Lord.

Reconciliation must come before Revival can take place.

Another example I recall took place in Moore Haven, where I was asked to speak at the First Baptist Church by their pastor, Teddy Greenberger. When I got there, the church was just permeated with a spirit of heaviness and division. When I stood up to preach, I had to tell them, "I'm sorry, but I cain't preach to y'all. There's too much fussin and fightin among yourselves and you all need to get right with each other before we can get started."

I didn't know what else to do but sit down and wait to be escorted out of the building, but after a long silence people began to get up one by one, and reconcile with each other. A sweet sense of the Holy Spirit began to fill that place, and before long revival broke out! I didn't even get a chance to "preach" – Thank the Lord - He does such a better job at it than me!

THE HOUND OF HEAVEN
TRACKS DOWN THE TOWN DRUNK

One night when we were having a prayer meeting at the Camp, the men told me about Erskin White. They said, "You know, Mickey, there's an old man in jail in Ft. Pierce. He's a good hearted old man - a harmless pan-handler. He sleeps in a refrigerator box down on the river by the fish house. He'll get out of jail in the morning and be back that night. He's going to die if he doesn't get help." So we took up an offering among the men. There was $35. That was a bunch of money for alcoholics to give. I sent a couple men into Ft. Pierce to pick Erskin up and pay his fine.

When they got there, the jailer just laughed at them. "You boys are crazy. If you take that ole man out in those woods he'll beat you back here and be drunk before you can get back to town."

But that jailer was wrong. Shortly after he got to the Camp, Erskin got saved. He had a complete transformation. A couple months later when he got ready to leave he said, "I'm going back to Ft. Pierce, Mickey, and I'm going to tell all the drunks and even the jailers about Jesus. There's no need for them to try to hide from me because I know all the hiding places."

He did return to Ft. Pierce and became a painter. He married, had a nice wife, a home and a little paint contracting business. I saw him on the street one day and called out to him. He came over to me with a wide grin and said, "Mickey, I just got thrown out of a bar..... for preaching!" He had been thrown out many times for being drunk, but this was his first time for sharing the Gospel, and he was tickled as could be.

He often returned to Dunklin for Friday night services but never on Sunday. He attended a local church in Ft.

Pierce on Sundays. But one Sunday morning I didn't have a message prepared and was out in the pasture praying for an idea when the Lord spoke to me real plain. "I don't want you to preach. Erskin White will preach." Erskin had never preached a sermon outside of the bars that I knew of. But sure enough, when I walked back up to the church, Erskin was there. I said, "Erskin, what are you doing here?" "The Lord told me to come out here this morning." "Well, the Lord told me you are going to preach," I said. He said, "All right." But when he got up to preach, he told everybody, "I came out here tonight to wash Bro. Mickey's feet. The Bible says we should do that."

I wasn't sure what to do, so one of the boys went out and got a pan of water, and that dear old soul washed my feet. It was a very humbling experience. It just tore me to pieces.

"Bro. Mickey taught us about the prodigal son being in the hog pen, and dear brothers, I want the whole world to know that I don't want any more of the hog pen!"

~ Erskin White

Chapter 13: Pioneers of the Past

DMC BOARD OF DIRECTORS AND TRUSTEES

Our First Board of Directors

On August 8, of 1963, T.W. Conley donated his services to draw up the Charter for a Christian non-profit corporation and Dunklin Memorial Camp became "an official legal entity." Charles McDougald, Al Cross, George Liner, Thomas Nix, Jack Williamson, Frank "Sonny" Williamson, Jr., Ernest Campbell, Sonny Holland served as our first Board of Directors. (not pictured: Adrian Rogers)

Dunklin has been blessed over the years by outstanding men and women who have served on our board. Their guidance and dedication have kept the program "on course" and moving forward.

They are men and women of integrity who have sacrificed time away from their busy lives in selfless service to the work of the Lord carried on at Dunklin.

Their tireless efforts on behalf of the men in the program and the staff have made a tremendous difference in the success of the ministry.

Pictured on these pages are only a fraction of those who have served our community in this capacity. A more extensive list is found in the "Dunklin Dignitaries"section.

Guy Strayhorn
Ft. Myers

Jack Williamson
Okeechobee

Frank Tillis
Pahokee

Ray Boggs
Deerfield

Charles McDuogald
Basinger

Evans Crary, Jr.
Stuart

Ralph Crews
Pahokee

Dr. Bill Cheshire
Pompano

J.S. Barwick
Pahokee

Bob Moody
Mulberry

Mallory Johnson
Stuart ...

Lovel Hitzing
Ft. Myers

Testimony of Francis and Ray Boggs

"Starting our life together in 1941, we thought we had the necessary sufficiency and strength in ourselves for the future. I was a Pilot in the Air Force and as far as the world was concerned, we were on top.

We both had accepted Christ as our Savior at an early age and though salvation was all that there was to being a Christian. We did not understand and enter into this new life as Jesus Christ intended for us to enjoy it. We lived in the world and thought we were happy. We started our family of five children, enjoying the life of carnal Christians. After a few years I became an alcoholic and subjected my wife, Frances, and children to ten years of living hell. As I became more involved in alcohol, Frances turned more and more to Jesus. She never gave up hope that our Lord would perform a miracle and take the alcoholic problem out of my life. When I had given up all hope and was scared of going to Hell, I fell on my knees and cried to Jesus to help me...and He did. Praise the Lord! He answered my prayer in 1955. Two years later I joined the church Frances and our children belonged to. Again as a carnal Christian. I went to work doing most everything from being the janitor to becoming an elected deacon.

Through prayer and study, we began to realize there was more to Christianity than we had experienced.

Involvement in Lay Witness Missions brought us into contact with some Christians who were sharing Jesus with others in an open and honest way, witnessing with boldness and power, and letting Jesus use them as vessels to perform miracles in His name. We wanted to be a part of this. In sharing with other Christians we discovered when we received Christ, we received potentially all that God had for us because He has no blessings outside of Christ. The indwelling and filling of the Holy Spirit is not an optional addendum, or a sort of extra blessing to salvation, it is an integral part. We had not entered into salvation as God intended for us to enjoy it. We were living beneath our privilege as a believer and not enjoying the abundant life. It was so simple, we had not asked Jesus for it all. So at a Lay Witness meeting in November 1971, we committed our lives fully to Jesus, asking for all that He had for us. From that moment on our lives have never been the same. Every day is an exciting adventure for us because we know the reality of being filled with the Holy Spirit and trying to live constantly, moment by moment under His control. We are learning how to walk in the Spirit and in this walking there is power unlimited.

In April 1971, we met Mickey and Laura Maye Evans from Dunklin Memorial Camp in Okeechobee, and were invited to coordinate their first Lay Witness weekend at the Camp. From that first encounter, we have been drawn to the Camp and their ministry. When Laos Institute, a part of Dunklin Memorial Camp, opened in April 1972, we committed our weekends to the ministry there.

We know that Jesus is with us now not just in natural power but supernatural, and not just in natural things that man can do but in supernatural things God alone can do. We are glad that we have kept our appointment with God."

The Boggs served the Camp faithfully for many years, and eventually their son Rich also joined the staff with his wife Cheri. Rich and Cheri helped foster an environment of contemplative prayer and led several hundred retreats the Camp. Rich also managed the kitchen and Cheri worked at the front desk, where her smile cheered everyone who came through the door. Cheri's severe case of scoliosis made it difficult for her to walk and eventually affected her breathing - ultimately taking her life. But she never let her condition steal her joy, and the Christ-like attitude she adopted toward her suffering left a profound impact on us all. Cheri left her earthly shell here behind at Dunklin, but we know she has never stopped rejoicing with Jesus.

Cheri and Richard Boggs

Testimony of Hugh and Corene Geiger

I wandered in sin for forty years, with no direction and no purpose to my life. I was an alcoholic. Two years ago at Dunklin Memorial Camp, I called on God and He saved me. Praise God, He gave me direction for my life. It was as if a huge, strong arm reached down and picked me up out of the pit of hell and loved me.

For the first time in my life, I found what I had been searching for all my life. He called me His son, and I called Him my Father. I have a burning desire in my heart to seek God's will for my life. I'm not yet what I want to be, but praise His Holy Name, I'm not what I used to be!

"Uncle Hugh", or simply "Unk", as he was affectionately known, got tired of the men breaking the shovel handles, so he decided to do something about it.

He took off the wood handles, and had iron pipes welded to all the implements.

After digging holes for a while with fifteen pound shovels, it was the men who were tired!

Bro. Paul Moore's Testimony

"As I sit here tonight, thanking Jesus for all the blessings that have been mine for the past fourteen months, my only regret is that I didn't let Him come into my heart before then. Most of you have read my testimony about my past in a previous edition of the Campfire, and that testimony was, for the most part, bad. But praise the Lord, since April 24, 1971, I have a testimony that is nothing but good.

Starting at that date, I was reborn, a completely new person. I confessed my sins, and I repented for them, and I was forgiven them by Jesus Christ, who died on the cross for me and my sins.

Sure, I have had some trials and tribulations, but the way I look at them, it is the Devil testing me and my faith in the Lord. As I was operated on, for cancer of the throat, in December of last year, the doctors didn't give me much of a chance to survive. But I was not afraid, I had Jesus with me, and I came through that operation with absolutely no trouble at all. After I came out of the intensive care unit, I did not have to take one sedative for pain, through the entire time of recuperation. That was God's way of showing me that He was right there with me. After leaving the hospital, I was unable to talk, so I prayed for His help to overcome this. My prayers were answered, for in less than two months from the time of the operation, I was talking. You see, He told me I would talk, and I did.

During this period, many, many wonderful and glorious things happened to me. Jesus has stayed right with me, and He has shown me new friends and some very special ones. "My, my, how could all these lovely and wonderful things happen to me?," I wonder, then I know they could only happen because of my Lord and Savior, Jesus Christ.

When everything was going so nice, that old Devil popped up again. He was trying out my faith for a second time. On May 25, I had to return to the hospital for another operation. This time, it was not quite as serious, but at the same time, bad enough. But Jesus was with me still, and Satan didn't stand a chance. My faith in Jesus has grown double -fold.

I want now, to tell all of you about the great miracles Jesus has performed in just the fourteen months of my salvation. He has saved my life on two occasions, He has let me talk again, He has let me come in contact with some of the most wonderful brothers and sisters in His whole Kingdom, but most important of all, He has saved my soul. Praise God, Praise His Holy Name. May God bless each and every one of you, as much as He has me.

A Poem by Paul

Once I was going down a lonely road,
just like a tired team with a heavy load.
And then I met Jesus, and I did not falter;
at Dunklin Memorial Camp down at the altar
It was such a great feeling, or so it seems
that it was like a great and wonderful dream,
But as I look back and begin to shout
I have really found Jesus, there is no doubt.
As I knelt there with brothers, Austin and Mickey,
I prayed to God to forgive my sins, just as quickly my past
vanished,
I could see Christ on the cross, dying for me.
As time passed on and my faith expanded,
my life I gave to Him and did as He commanded
I remain here at the Camp,
to minister to men
Who like myself,
think they have come to the end
So worship the Lord,
and thank Him
for your blessings
they outnumber by far,
all of the messings.
And praise the Lord
with one big yell
For saving our souls
from going to hell!

The Cross fountain between the office and Good Sam building was built by men in the program as a memorial to alumni and staff member Paul Moore "as a symbol of the love that flowed so freely from his life".

Chapter :14
Saints Still Here

Dr. Bob Crowe,
President Dunklin
Ministry Training
School

In 1956, I was attending Seminary in New Orleans when the Salk vaccine was first released to prevent the dreaded disease of polio. The state of Louisiana had concerns about the safety of the vaccine and held off distribution to the public. My wife, Millie, contracted polio and died. I was left with two children under the age of three. I returned home to south Florida and took a position at the church in Key Largo.

One day my aunt who was living with me taking care of the children said, "Bob, you need to get married again. Silvia Felton would make you a good wife and mother to your children.

Sylvia was eighteen years old, one of the teenagers in our congregation.

I began to think about that and then to pray about it. One morning I prayed, "Lord, if you want me to ask Sylvia Felton to be my wife, let it rain before I go to bed tonight." That evening I was reading and had forgotten about my prayer. I put my book down and went to the door to turn off the porch light preparing to go to bed ... and noticed it was raining. Then I remembered.

The next day some of the college kids, Sylvia and I were playing monopoly at their home. When finished I asked Sylvia if she would like to go to a friend's house to plan the Christmas Program. I pulled over at the Post Office a mile from her home and told her what had God had shown me. When I proposed marriage to her she quickly said "Yes". (She had been praying for her future mate since she was 14 years old. God told her that I was the One the first time she saw me).

We had been married five years and were ministering at North Side Church in Miami.   One day I drove up to visit Adrian Rogers at Park View Baptist Church in Ft. Pierce.   Adrian and I had attended Stetson University in Deland, Florida together and seminary in New Orleans. When I walked in his office, he was on his knees with Mickey Evans looking at something on the floor. I said, "What are you guys looking at?"

Mickey said, "We're looking at a map of land for an alcoholic rehabilitation center the Lord wants built."

I said, "Oh." They had an aerial photo map spread out on the floor beneath them. It looked like mostly swamp. "Is the land for sale?" I asked.

"No," said Mickey. "Well, do you have any money?" I pressed.

"No," he answered.   I said, "How are you going to do that?"

"The Lord just told me to do it," Mickey answered simply.

When we started the tent meetings we had people coming from all over. One time it was cold, and they put a smudge pot in the tent to kind of warm up the place.

It began to smoke. It got so smoky in the tent we all had to get out. While we were standing outside waiting for the smoke to clear, a blind man began to prophesy over the land.

He said "You can't see it, but I can see the buildings. There is going to be a tabernacle over here, dormitories over there and people will come."

It was a fantastic time. We had pastors like Sonny Holland, Bud Unger, Jeff Styles, Peter Lord and Adrian Rogers. Every Friday I came up to teach Bible classes Friday afternoon, night and Saturday. Then we would go back to my church in Miami for Sunday services. It was exciting. We had powerful preaching, and people were being saved.

For several years we traveled back and forth. Sylvia, wanted to move to the Camp, but there was no place to live. Many weekends we stayed in a little pup tent.

The first tabernacle they built here had no floor - just dirt with straw on it. Old benches to sit on.

One day I drove up to the camp and saw a football sailing over the trees. I asked around to find out who had kicked that ball so high. Somebody said, "That was Billy Lamb. He's the worst man in Okeechobee County. He almost killed a man with his bare hands. He's separated from his wife, Nadine. He's been in most of the drunk tanks and drug rehab places around." Billy was over 6'5" and stocky.

Saturday morning while teaching my class I said, "God speaks, and he's spoken to every one of you."

After the class, Billy came up to me and said, "Preacher, during my quiet time this morning I was along the road, and I think God was talking to me."

I said, "Billy, do what He says."

That night we had a service, and when the altar call was given Billy went up to the altar and received Jesus.

Sonny Holland, a preacher from Ft. Pierce, was there, and he came up and put his arm around Billy. Billy got real mad, turned red in the face, pushed Sonny's arm off and stormed outside. I decided I better go after him. When I caught up with him, I said, "Billy, the devil told you to get out, didn't he?" He said, "I dunno who it was, but these preachers are buggin' me. I'm gettin' outta here."

I said, "Okay, but you'll be back. You can run, but the Lord is going to catch you."

He said, "I'm not ever comin' back!"

I prayed, "Lord, you're going to have to send some mighty big angels to bring Billy back!"

The following morning Mickey was teaching and I saw him glance toward the door. I turned and saw Billy come in. He sat beside me and said, "I tried to get away, preacher. I don't know what I'm doin' here." I just grinned and thanked the Lord for those big angels.

All kinds of amazing things were happening at the Camp. People from all walks of life were being saved: a medical doctor who had lost his practice, his wife, his money; a professor of Philosophy from New York University, a man who was heir to the Philco fortune. He got saved and later became the president of a military academy. Lives were being changed.

One of the members of my church in Miami had a yardman working for her who was an alcoholic. She began talking with him about the Camp. He seemed a little interested because he was forty years old and had been an alcoholic all of his adult life. He had never owned anything. I talked to him and said, "Walt, I'd like to take you out to the Camp. We have a program that would help you."

"How much do they pay?" he asked.

"They don't pay you anything," I said.

"Well, I can't do that," he said.

I told him if he completed the program he may get an opportunity to get a better job. A lot of the men get jobs with the big farms in the area. "Well, I guess I could try it," he agreed.

The following morning I arrived fifteen minutes earlier than we had agreed on. He was just leaving his house. "I went out and got me a six-pack, and I've been drinking. I decided not to go. But since you're here, I guess I might as well go with you," he said.

He was at the camp about a month when he got hooked up with another guy and cooked up a scheme for writing bogus checks when they left the Camp. They were going to make a lot of money.

As the time approached for him to get out, the scheme began to bother Walt. He knew he was going to get in trouble. He went to Mickey and said, "Bro. Mickey, I don't think I'm ready to go." Mickey told him to stay as long as he needed to.

But Walt did not yet believe in God.

On Thanksgiving Day Mickey walked out in the woods and prayed that God would give us a dormitory to house the men. He told us that God spoke to his heart that we could start it that week. So we went out, cut four stakes

from a cabbage palm tree, marked off a 35x100 foot building and stretched string around it. We called all the men in the Camp to join us inside the designated spot for

Dorm Staked Out

prayer. We knelt on the ground and claimed it by faith.

Walt took me aside and said, "If God builds that dormitory I'll start believing. Until then I just don't believe."

The very next night while we were having our Friday Night Camp Meeting service we heard two big trucks pulling in the dirt road to the Camp.

We went outside and found them parked next to our string, loaded with enough concrete blocks to build a twenty-four bed dormitory! Eighteen hundred blocks were donated by King's Chapel, Vero Beach and Fairlawn Baptist church, Ft. Pierce.

We immediately started unloading the blocks and people started praising the Lord, crying and singing.

Blocks Arrived

Walt grabbed Mae Delle Murphy and said, "Let's go to the altar. I think I'm ready!" He gave his heart to the Lord and became a beautiful Christian. He got a job as a supervisor at one of the big farms, for the first time in his life he bought a truck and a home. God gave him a wife, and he became a deacon in a church in Okeechobee.

MRS. MAE DELLE MURPHY

Walt Jordan discing

One day while Walt was discing a pasture with the tractor he notice a huge rattlesnake, distracted by the snake he ran the tractor up on pine sapling and got it stuck. He wouldn't get off the tractor for fear the snake would bite him so there he sat until someone came and killed the snake. We ribbed him about letting a "little ole rattler" run him up a pine tree!

In 1966, I decided to leave my church in Miami, move my family to New Orleans, where I would return to school for my Masters Degree, and then to go into the Navy as a Chaplain. When we were at Dunklin saying goodbye to our friends, Mickey walked with me out under a big oak tree to pray and said, "I want you to promise me something." I said, "What's that?"

He said, "When you get through with school and the Navy, I want you to come back to Dunklin and teach." I agreed.

In the meantime....before I had even finished up my training, our country went to war and so I found myself on a plane headed to Viet Nam. When I got off, a Navy chief was standing next to me, and he said, "Boy, I don't know what's going on, but there is a lot of security around." About that time the explosions started. Rockets were coming in. He slapped me on the back and said, "Hit the dirt!

We were in the middle of the Tet Offensive. We were in the bunkers every night and slept with our gas masks on.

The first time the rockets came in, the phone rang in our bunker and someone said, "You and the doc get over to the sick bay. We got casualties!" That's when I really learned how to pray. I thank God for my time in the military and continue to pray for those who daily put their lives on the line for our freedom.

In 1994, upon retiring from my career in the Navy, Sylvia and I returned to Dunklin. Sylvia and I have a home on the campus not a stone's throw from that very same oak tree. She is involved in the intercessory prayer ministry and my primary job is teaching in our International Ministry Training School.

Today, the casualties I witness are a result of a spiritual war being fought on the front of addiction. I do my best to minister to the wounded and support the staff with the weapon of prayer.

Oliver Livingston (Red) Fox, Jr.

Completed the DMC program in 1965
Returned in 1981,Returned for good in 1984

The "Fox" and His Special Lady Friend, Theresa

TAP! TAP!

I raised my hurting head from the front seat of the car. TAP! TAP! It was a police officer trying to get my attention by tapping on the closed window. "Driver's License?" I fumbled around in my wallet and finally found it. "Where you from, Sir?"

"South Carolina – Charleston, to be exact.

"What are doing here in Florida?

Ah, well, ahhh....

"Your family in S.C. has an A.P.B. out on you. They want to know where you are. Get in my car. No Sir, not the front seat - the back seat." It was then I learned that police car's back doors do not open from the inside.

KNOCK! KNOCK!

Next stop - Titusville Jail. The charge: Vagrancy

Me? A success all my life? A vagrant?!

As I sat in the bullpen, I began to take inventory: a six-hundred mile trip, one week …and a half? I didn't remember. Ten cents in my pocket, a paycheck stub for $800, tie askew, sport coat crumpled, shirt collar black with dirt, smelly, ugly beard, bloodshot eyes, shaky hands, wife gone, child gone, home gone, and all my friends avoiding me. Me a success? Well maybe not. KNOCK! KNOCK!

"Fox, Red Fox?" the jailer called. "You have a visitor." Dave was his name. A person I had never met, a Christian friend of my ex-wife. "Having problems?" Yes. "Feel like getting out of jail?" Yes.
"You want some help?" Yes.
"Will you go to a place in Okeechobee where you can get help?" Um…..I guess so.

Next stop: twenty miles into nowhere. Dunklin Memorial Camp, a rehab joint for drunks. I still wasn't quite ready to admit I was one.

Two days later: Man! What am I doing in this desolate place with a bunch of drunks and crazy Christians? Me, the successful and smart Red Fox? Then this Bible verse came to my mind from out of nowhere. *"But God hath chosen the foolish things of the world to confound the wise; and God hath chosen the weak things of the world to confound the things which are mighty."*
KNOCK! KNOCK!

These Christians, these peculiar people, began working with me, not just on my alcoholic problem, but on other areas of my life: projections, denial, impulsiveness, evasion, frustration, helplessness, ambivalence, manipulation, remorse, low self-esteem, rationalization, hostility and dependence. They treated my character faults with two medicines: infinite patience and infinite love.
KNOCK! KNOCK!

Who's there? Oh, it's you, Lord. Yes, I was just thinking back and telling this person about the miracle you worked in my life through your people. Maybe you can work one in their life, too. Thank you for the opportunity to tell them, Lord.

I've always told Bro. Mickey he has to be here to preach my funeral, because he never says anything bad about me. That will keep the funeral service short and make everybody happy!

I was raised in North Charleston, SC and went in the army for four years. Came out and went to the Citadel. When I graduated I went to work at Cape Canaveral in Florida and worked there five and a half years.

The first time I came to Dunklin was in 1965. I had been working at the Cape since 1959, started drinking too much, lost my job, wife, kids, home..... the usual.

When my ex-wife's friend got me out of jail and brought me to Dunklin, I thought I was going on vacation. A nice spa. Beaches, etc. I was just happy to get out of jail. I stayed at the Camp about a year, left to do field research and came back in '81. I was up and down with the longest period of sobriety lasting maybe 3 years.

When I came back the second time, there was a guy here named Mike Cole whose father owned a bakery in Hendersonville, NC and had donated bakery equipment, a large oven with rotating shelves to make our own bread. Mike was working himself to death, so I started helping him. We made what bread the Camp could use, and sold some in town and at the Emmaus Walks.

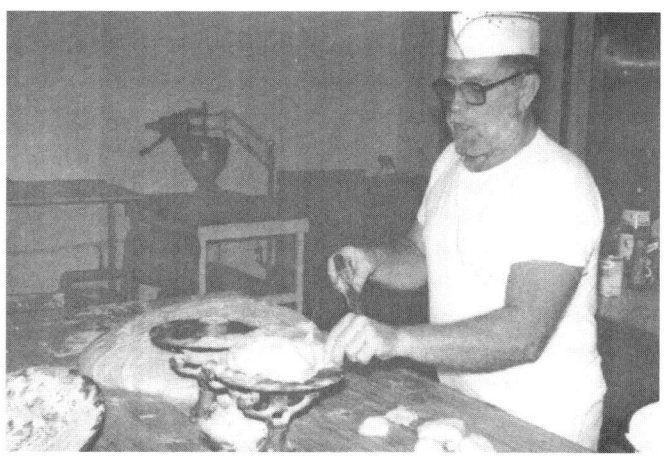

Mike got married and left, so I was the bread maker for a while.

When I got tired of that and left the Camp again, I moved to California and lasted about 8 months. I called Mickey and asked him if I could come home. He said "of course, we've missed you."

He's a compassionate man, but sort of stupid too, because he sent me the money to come back to Dunklin. To keep from falling apart on the five-day bus ride back to Florida, I went to the liquor store and bought something to sip along the way.

I guess maybe Mickey knew what he was doing after all, because when the bus passed through New Orleans, I was tempted to get off. But I knew if I got in that town I'd never get out...... and I had that bottle to sip on.

The third time I came back to Dunklin was the charm. I lived in the dorm four years, because they didn't know what to do with me. They said, "He's not leaving, and we can't afford him. What are we gonna do with him?"

At that time old Uncle Hugh was managing all the maintenance on the place. I assisted him. When he died they broke up the different jobs, and I started taking care of the electrical, plumbing, household appliances, refrigeration, air conditioning - things like that. I'm on duty most of the time, but I can refuse. If someone's shower quits working at night, I tell them to go next door.

They all say, "Don't wake Red up when he's asleep!" That's the persona I try to cultivate. But my bark is worse than my bite. Most of the time I have two guys assigned to my team. Once in awhile I tell them we're going on an archeological dig - to find an underground pipe or something. I know most of the Camp, but there are still some things unknown to me.

About the time I think I've found a man to take over my responsibilities, so I can retire and get some rest, they leave to start their own ministries!

It's really nice living out here. I've been here quite a while now, and I have good friends. God is good to all of us. The other day I was driving Mickey someplace, and as we were leaving the Camp he was telling me a story about something. He finished, and then a few miles down the road he started telling me the same story again. He got about half way through it and stopped and said, "Didn't I just tell you that?!" I laughed.

"If Red Fox ever leaves Dunklin I'm going too, because the whole place is going to fall apart." ~ Mickey

Liz and Dave Lide

"Dave and I started coming to the Camp in 1971 when we still lived in Sarasota. At that time, we were part of a Lay Renewal group, and came to the Camp several times over the years for retreats. I told someone once that we had slept in almost every room in what is now the office. Those weekends were memorable because we both had been recently baptized in the Holy Spirit, and appreciated so much being with like-minded people. Reid Hardin was leader of the group, and had many wonderful speakers. I remember at one time sitting on the floor in a small group, in the office which Laura Maye now uses. She was asking us to plot our lives on a blackboard. When it came my turn, I drew a swathe across the board, saying "All my life I have been pushed into doing things" and from that time on I have been free--a freedom to do what the LORD wants me to do, to the best I can. Dave was on the Board for about two years, then we moved to North Carolina, staying 16 years, but spending a number of summers at the Camp, two years even trailering Dave's Ultralight plane--that was some experience with the washboard road. We loved being here-Dave had 12 years of heart disease. Finally Mickey said move here, because every time Dave leaves he gets sick. We made the move in

1971, and he died in 1973, with Mickey in the room in Miami Jackson Hospital singing Amazing Grace. How precious to me. Since, I have been working at the office and enjoying the men with whom I work. That will soon come to an end, because I will be living with Hamp and Jennifer and the girls in Palm Bay, FL. You better pray for them! I'm going to miss all my wonderful friends here so much, but all Praise and Glory be to God Our Father, and The Lord Jesus Christ Who gave me the gift of Salvation and forgives me daily. I love you all". Liz

Wilbur and Mary Lanier

I don't even remember when I first knew Bro. Mickey - long before I had any remembrance.

We were in school together back in the '40s right there in Okeechobee. It was a cow town and fishing hub then.

That's what Wilbur's family did - they cat-fished for a living. They built little huts, chickees, over on a lake, and they would live in that and fish until they weren't catching anything. Then they'd move on to another lake and do the same thing. Later on they'd come back to the first lake. Wilbur said many times they'd move back in the same chickee. Sometimes other people would be using it, and they'd just go over to the other side of the lake and build another one.

They made their beds out of (Spanish) moss. Took a burlap bag and put moss in it to sleep on. They also hunted, and sold frogs and turtles.

My family moved to Okeechobee when I was two years old from Savannah, Georgia. My aunt came first and the rest of the family followed. Franklin J. Camp, my grandpa, was a Methodist preacher, and one day my aunt asked him, "Papa, don't you believe you should seek the Lord for the Baptism of the Holy Spirit?"
She had recently had this experience.

He said, "Sister, I don't really know if I need to or not, but I'll ask the Lord and if He shows me I'll let you know." A little while later he said, "Yes, I believe I do." So he sought the Lord and received the Baptism and became a

Church of God minister. He was a quiet, humble, meek little old man.

Wilbur and I took children in at our home in Okeechobee. We raised thirty-three children - two of our own and thirty-one foster children. We raised twelve to what I would call grown

I got Martha when she was four years old. There were six children in the family, and I got five of them. One stayed with an aunt. Martha is now forty-three and still lives with me and helps out here at the Camp. She is such a blessing to me, and everyone she knows. I don't know what I'd do without her.

Wilbur made $250 a week, and at one point we had eleven children in the house. We never knew how we made ends meet, but somehow we did. When it was time to start school, and one of the kids didn't have clothes, a friend would come by with a big brown grocery bag full of clothes and say, "My little boy just out-grew these. Can you use them?" That would out-fit one of my little boys to go to school. That's the way things happened.

One time the roof on our house in Okeechobee started leaking, and I don't know yet how Mickey found out about it. But he sent a man over to give an estimate on fixing it, and he put a new roof on our house. He sure did that thing! He used to send five or ten pound bags of hamburger to town for us once in a while.

Mickey has always had a lot on his plate, but if somebody comes by starting a new ministry, he'll say, "How can I help?" That's God in Mickey. What he gives out, God replenishes.

One day my sister-in-law said, "Mary, are you crazy? You're taking all these kids and using up everything Wilbur makes to live now. What are you going to do when Wilbur retires?"

I figured if we did what God told us to do as we went along and lived one day at the time, He would take care of us when that time comes.

And He did.

When it came time for Wilbur to retire, he went downtown to sign up for his Social Security. Mickey met up with him and said, "Mr. Wilbur, when you get ready to retire I've got some dragline work out at the camp I'd like for you to come out and help us with." So in 1985 Wilbur started working out here. The kids and I would come for the Friday night services and the Gospel sings and fish-fries on the weekends. That was my daddy's joy - to come out here on the weekends. At the beginning of Mickey's ministry, I went along with him sometimes to the jails and ministered and sang to the prisoners. They even let the prisoners come out here to Dunklin from Belle Glade Prison on the weekends. Austin Brown was one of those, and he still came back to Dunklin to visit and give his testimony to the boys in the program until the Lord took him home to glory..

Several years later we sold our house in town and moved out here. When I asked for this house, they told me the termites were holding hands to hold it up. I said the Holy Spirit can call the angels to hold hands and hold it up better, so they fixed it up and allowed us to move in.

I didn't realize until years later how living in this house would give me a ministry with the boys in the program. Wilbur and I were out here several years before I ever ministered to anybody. I worked in the canning plant and haberdashery, went to prayer groups and things like that, but I didn't have an opportunity to minister directly to the men.

But one day, the Lord just opened it up for the guys to begin to come by my house, and come in when they felt like they needed a little visit from a grandma.

Over half of them go by this house twice a day on their way to work and coming back. They pass this house four times a day. I can usually look at their shoulders and tell what kind of shape they're in - if their head is bowed, or if they're angry or if they're just struttin' their stuff, I've seen them all those ways right out these windows.

If one of them feels down from something that has happened, I don't sympathize with him. I tell him the good that God can work out of it. Anything that happens to him God is allowing in his life to grow him. I don't teach any condemnation or say they're justified for feeling bad at anybody. All I do is show them a grandma's love and give them a cold soda. I love them, but I don't feel sorry for them, or take up for them. When my kids got in trouble I never took up for them against the authorities. That's not the way to help them.

They go through a lot when they come here. They have to make the decision every day to stay here, and to give their heart to the Lord. I pray for them. Sometimes they make the wrong decision, and when they walk out of the Camp, my heart goes with them.

I have a stack of their pictures up here on my lamp, and every now and then I look at them and pray over them. I ask the Lord to take care of them wherever they are, and if they can't come back here to get them somewhere for help.

One little fella sat right on my couch just like a little bantam rooster. He had it all under control. He knew who he was and what he was supposed to be doing, and these people out here didn't know. He thought the world owed him. One day he decided to walk. I called his wife and told her we're not gonna give up on him. Where there's breath, there's hope. We'll just keep praying for him.

When they complete the program at Dunklin, it's like they are fresh-poured concrete. It's a good foundation, but if you try to build on green concrete it ain't going to stand. You have got to give concrete time to set-up before you can build on it. Sometimes you need Stage II, SLT or something out there that is going to continue to grow and season you.

Sometimes I see them, and their concrete is so green - maybe like the day it was poured!   But they think they can take on the world. I tell them, "The enemy is out there like a big alligator ready to take his tail and slap you flat on your face if you don't stick with your journaling, your quiet time with the Lord and your walking right."

I'm embarrassed that I can't get around too well, but in my heart, spirit, and strength, I don't feel any different than I did when I was forty. I can see and hear. I can see spiritually what God is doing around me. Maybe He is using me to show people that even when you're in pain, and God is not fixing things, you still keep going and hold on to Him. That's what I do.

Laura Maye's grandma went to the same church I went to in Okeechobee years ago, Aunt Jenny Campbell. She was very old, but she was faithful to God. Even though she couldn't hear or sing she still went to church and showed her faithfulness to the end.   Dunklin is a good place to live. All my life I've loved being in the country, having big oak trees around, and looking out over a lake. And here I am, eighteen miles from town with big shady oaks around my house and Lake Elijah in my back yard. And when Wilbur passed away Mr. Hugh (Murrow) and his wife invited me and Martha to dinner one night and told me, "Miss Mary, if there is ever anything you need, just let me know." He is a busy man, but no matter how busy he is, he will give me a hug and ask, "Is everything all right?"

My biological son and his wife asked us to come live with them, but I told them we have a good home. And God has a job for us to do yet.

"These gatekeepers… were responsible for guarding the entrance to the house of the Lord, the house that was formerly at tent."

I Chronicles 10:23

Miss Martha and Aunt Mary

Miss Mary's Brother Kell Hood and his wife Joyce have shared their smiles and hugs with us for many years.

Nell and Gene Williams

In 1962, my husband, Gene, and I heard Mickey preach a revival in Ft. Pierce and tell about his vision for the Camp. Some years later my brother in law, Ralph Crews, joined Dunklin's Board of Directors, and in 1979 our son, Michael, had a drinking problem and went through the program.

We began attending the Friday Night Meetings at Dunklin, and Mickey and Gene soon became friends. Since Gene was in construction, and Mickey needed a builder and machinery, he asked us to be on staff.

I had talked with some of the women who lived at the remote Camp and knew it was a hard life. I said, "There is no way I am living out there!" Then I was making the bed one morning, and God spoke to me as clear as I'm sitting here, "The Camp is not for you. It is for Gene." So we moved to Dunklin.

Gene got saved, and he and our son baptized each other in Lake Elijah. It is one of my most precious memories.

Before I really knew Laura Maye, I became friends with her mother, Stella. I sat many an hour next to her, talking and listening to her tell about the Camp and about Laura Maye. That's when the Lord gave me a special love for Laura Maye ... before I even got to know her.

If Laura Maye and Mickey were in conflict over something, Ma Campbell would take his side, because she knew he was right. Laura Maye would say, "Mickey's so stubborn. I can't tell him anything!"

Her mother would say, "If Mickey wasn't stubborn he wouldn't have stayed here as long as he has." That was true. Mickey had to have determination to stick with it and fulfill God's vision. I imagine he wanted to leave a few times, and he may have wanted to die a time or two, but he isn't through yet. Gene and I became good friends with Mickey and Laura Maye, laughing, praying and crying together over the years. The first of many vacations with Laura Maye and Mickey was for a week on a friend's yacht to the Bahamas. We had a wonderful time - sat on the deck each morning watching the sun on the water, had church on the boat, snorkeled together every day.

Mickey wanted to cut the week short to be home in time for Sunday church services at Dunklin, but Laura Maye wanted to finish the full week. Each morning Mickey would ask her, "Honey, what day is it?"

So, middle of the week I suggested she tell him it was Tuesday instead of Wednesday. "He won't fall for that!" she said. "He's not stupid," and we got tickled at the thought of this little deception. We laughed and had a good time with it. But she tried it, and it worked.

When Sunday morning rolled around, we were heading across the Gulf Stream, miles from the Florida east coast.

Gene and Nell Williams

Mickey turned on the radio and heard what day it was and called down to us, "Laura Maye, you said it was Saturday!"

Later that same day a bad thunder storm came up, and then something happened to the fuel line on the boat, cutting the engine. We bounced around out in the Gulf Stream for hours with lightening flashing and driving rain while the guys tried to fix the problem. They finally called the Coast Guard and had us towed in. By that time we had drifted miles north of where we should have been. Mickey said it was our fault for having us out there on a Sunday!

I worked in the office with Laura Maye for ten years. Many times over the years she and I would be paying bills, making ends meet and trying to balance the checkbook right to the penny. Mickey would come in and say, "Laura Maye, we need to send a check to support the work in Guatemala. Make it out for $350." She would remind him we didn't have any extra money.

"Don't worry about it. The Lord will provide," he would say. Then when the mail came, there would be a check for that amount. It happened over and over. We were never late with a bill. Never owed anybody past due. It was amazing.

We started a women's program for a short time. The girls weren't all alcoholics. Several were recently divorced and devastated by it, one was anorexic. Several women living at the camp at the time helped handle the girls, but Laura Maye was the only trained counselor. We found that women require more counseling than men. They were mostly young, emotional, and have more physical problems than men. It turned out to be more than we were prepared to handle, and it was discontinued.

At that time we had only twenty-five men in the program. We often loaded up the guys and the staff and went fishing over on the C-23 Canal or to the rim canal at Port Mayaca.

One old man, Hugh Geiger, went through the program and then stayed on for six years as the grounds keeper. He lived alone in a small trailer and stayed to himself, so nobody was aware that he had started drinking again. Eventually he was found out, and Mickey told Gene to take Hugh to the bus and send him home.

The next thing we knew he was back. Laura Maye and Laurie had found him drunk behind the grocery store in Indiantown and brought him back to the Camp. He cleaned up again, married Laura Maye's aunt and worked with the men in the citrus and palm tree groves for years.

Uncle Hugh's Testing Grounds

He was rough on them. But at graduation time when the men stood up to give their testimonies, they all loved Uncle Hugh. It must have been because he was real, and they knew it.

Christie, Katie, Hugh, Sarah and Emily Murrow

Hugh Murrow, Camp Administrator

I came to Dunklin in March of 1984, with a very serious alcohol problem. Alcoholism had been rampant in my family and I was actually a third generation alcoholic. I received Jesus as my Lord and Savior here and my life was never the same again. He delivered me from the craving of alcohol. He accomplished a tremendous healing and gave me a divine purpose for my life. I have been blessed to be a part of the ministry here for the past 28 years. It has been an honor to serve the Lord here and watch Him perform miracles in other men's lives as He did in mine. I have had the privilege to be mentored by Brother Mickey and it has been a blessing to walk with him and serve him during this time. In 1987, the Lord brought me a beautiful Christian wife. Christie and I have had three daughters, Katie, Sarah, and Emily, who grew up here at Dunklin. I know of no better place to raise a family than in a Christian community like Dunklin. I could not have dreamed of a better life than the one that God has blessed me with here. It is only by His grace and mercy that I live today, and have received the many blessings He has given over these years. I thank the Lord for His goodness and I thank Brother Mickey and Laura Maye for their obedience and faithfulness in fulfilling the vision that the God gave them.

Christy Murrow, R.N.

I've had the privilege of being a part of Dunklin for the past 25 years, and what changes there have been! Little did I know what I was becoming a part of when I became Hugh's wife. We've seen the program grow, the housing and community expand, and through it we've raised our daughters here and watched them grow up as well. Living in the swamp has had its interesting moments, but having been raised as a missionary kid on a compound in India, I see now how God was preparing me to live in this very unique place.

Being a staff wife here at the Camp has brought its own distinctive delights and challenges. My primary ministry these past years has been to our family, and to the staff wives. Bringing up three girls here has provided for some different moments, but our family has been the richer for it. We have learned firsthand the abundance of Christian community and being part of the Dunklin family. I've been blessed with dear friends who've become sisters, and have a wealth of wise men and women who, through the years, have taught, listened, encouraged, mentored and spoken to the truth in love to me. It hasn't always been easy, but it's been good!

As God has called out staff to birth new ministries or move on to different places, there have been many difficult goodbyes. That has been the hardest part of living here. The good part is we have lots of special people to visit! God has used this place to bring healing and wholeness, and to demonstrate His love and faithfulness time and time again, to not only me, but countless others. It has been a privilege to see marriages restored, families reconciled and our single guys find the wife of God's choosing and go on to raise families that honor Him. I am blessed and grateful to have been chosen to be a part of such a special ministry and place.

Chapter 15:
Jewels from the Devil's Junkpile

"And the Lord will give you a new name.
The Lord will hold you in His hands for all to see –
a splendid crown in the Hands of God."
Isaiah 62:3

Jewels from the Devil's Junk Pile

Song by Larry J. Ries (Florida State Prison)

One drink without an end,
Nights without a day;
The end was one last shot
Somewhere down the way.
Once lost without a hope,
Left without a dream;
The end could be but death,
That's the way it seemed.
That's when Jesus came
And walked the second mile
And saved yet one more jewel
From the devil's junk pile.
Once life was in a bottle,
Death was waiting there
'Til a voice whispered low,
"My friend, Someone cares."
That's why Jesus came
And walked here for awhile,
And He's still saving jewels
From the devil's junk pile.

"The Addict's Psalm"

"Oh give thanks unto the Lord, for he is good: for his mercy endureth forever. Let the redeemed of the Lord say so, whom he hath redeemed from the hand of the enemy; And gathered them out of the lands, from the east, and from the west, from the north, and from the south. They wandered in the wilderness in a solitary way; they found no city to dwell in. Hungry and thirsty, their soul fainted in them. Then the cried unto the Lord in their trouble, and he delivered them out of their distresses. And he led them forth by the right way, that they might go to a city of habitation. Oh that men would praise the Lord for his goodness, and for his wonderful works to the children of men! For he satisfieth the longing soul, and filleth the hungry soul with goodness. Such as sit in darkness and in the shadow of death, being bound in affliction and iron: because they rebelled against the words of God, and contemned the counsel of the most High; Therefore he brought down their heart with labor; they fell down, and there was none to help. Then they cried unto the Lord in their trouble, and he saved them out of their distresses. He brought them out of darkness and the shadow of death, and brake their bands in sunder. Oh that men would praise the Lord for his goodness, and for his wonderful works to the children of men!"

Psalm 107:1-15

"We don't have to look far to find Satan's Junkyard; it's all around us. Broken lives, broken hearts, wasted, misspent souls that are broken and bound by sin. The skid-rows of a thousand cities are filled with human derelicts who have ceased to care whether they live or die, life has lost all meaning to them. The jails and prisons of our country are overflowing with men and women who are bound outwardly by steel bars and inwardly by the even stronger fetters of sin; our newspapers are plastered with pictures of those who are too weak to keep up the wild pace of modern society."
Campfire, November 1971

"Then they that feared the Lord spoke often one to another: And the Lord hearkened, and heard it, and a book of remembrance was written before him for them that feared the Lord, and that thought upon his name. And they shall be mine, saith the Lord of Hosts, in that day when I make up my Jewels; And I will spare them, as a man spareth his own son that serveth him. Then shall ye return, and discern between him that serveth God and him that serveth him not." Malachi 3:16-18

When the Lord gathers His Jewels, praise God, we can rejoice that a big hand-full of them were picked up from the altars at Dunklin Memorial Camp. The lives of these men are a tremendous testimony to the power of our Lord Jesus Christ, to make Jewels from the Devil's Junkpile.

The Garcia Family

March 1976
Dear Brothers,
I want you all to know that when I first came to D.M.C. from Pahokee, I was an alcoholic and I didn't know the Lord. I was having big problems, and I was losing my family. We were getting farther and farther apart. But, thanks to the Lord, with the help of Brother Mickey and all the staff, I was able to get close to the Lord.
There have been trials and tribulations, but the Lord has always been there to lift me up. We are all together again as a family and I praise the Lord Jesus!
Juan Garcia

Maria and Juan Garcia

Johnnie Smith

When the doctor told me he could do nothing more for me, that I'd have to seek higher help, I was ready for almost anything. So like a drowning man grasping for straws, I came to Dunklin. Upon arriving, my first thoughts were, as many others were, I'm sure, "What a place." I thought I had been saved several years before, but then, way back in my mind, I knew that no one who cared for worldly, things, especially alcohol, the way I did, could possibly be saved. So there at the Camp, about the second or third week during Bible Study, I was like Saul when he was on the road to Damascus to persecute the Christian people. "I saw the light," and God saved an old sinner like me. Since then I've been trying to let my light shine, that others might see Jesus in me.

Johnnie and his son Frank Smith.

Arnold and Marie Hughes

For many years I told God He could have second place in my life. I didn't have time to spend with Him. I had my job and family to take care of. I thought the more I worked and brought home money for my family, that was all that counted. I'd work day and night and hardly ever had time to be with the family.

Physically I couldn't keep this up without a crutch. So alcohol became a real good crutch for me. Then I began to realize after eighteen and a half years of married life, it had really been a mess. My children no longer respected me, and neither did my wife. I could stop drinking for periods of time, but then I would always start back.

My whole family had prayed for me for so long, that it finally got to the point where God was really dealing with me. Then two of my brothers became very ill with cancer. In fact, one of them that I visited with in the hospital just a week before I came to Dunklin, was at death's door. God was telling me He wanted me to stop and look at my life. The very day that I went to the Camp, this brother started to get better. Miracles? Yes – I have seen them with my own eyes. My Lord is very much in the miracle working business today, as He was back when He walked on this earth.

Before I left Dunklin, this very brother visited me and told me just what the Lord had done for him.

That's just one of the miracles God has shown me.

God has truly been good to my family and me. My wife, Marie, my two daughters, Judy and Madonna, and my son, Johnny, will always have a special spot in our hearts for the staff members of D. M. C., for without their love and service for the Lord, we would never have been able to have a Christian family today.

The three months that I spent at the Camp will be a lasting memory for the rest of my life. God really works for those who will let Him. But we have to be willing to submit to Him, before He will take over our life. He will not push himself on us. One of the many things I learned is that it is easier to forgive others than it is to forgive yourself.

I pray God will show me just what His will for my life is. I've found out there is more to life than just working on a job and never having time for the Lord. Please pray for us that we might find the service in life that God has for us.

Arnold Hughes

The Value of Discipleship

February, 1984 By Joe Cordovano

Kelly and Joe Cordovano founded Fresh Start Ministry in Orlando after training at Dunklin.

A disciple is a pupil. It is someone taking you under their wing and teaching you everything they know about Christianity. It is crying with you when you hurt and rejoicing with you when you are blessed. It is the teacher not being afraid if you advance further than him in the ways of the Lord.

That sums up my view of the value of discipleship. It is invaluable – you can not possibly put a price on it.

What I would like to do is share something that I think shows exactly how valuable it is to me.

There is a lake called Elijah. It is a man-made lake which was made by works and also strategically placed by man for appearance and convenience. If we further look at this lake we see that although God had very little to do with it, He did ordain it. He uses it to water his cattle and irrigate the fields around it. He further uses it for the pleasure of His people here at the Camp and also for the Lord's work – as this is where people are baptized. If the lake is not taken care of, weeds and fungus will choke it out and it will not be as useful. Its beauty will fade and people won't be drawn to it because it will be overgrown with weeds.

God sends people to the lake who prune the trees, mow the grass and pull the weeds and before long it will be beautiful again. It becomes fruitful again. God's animals can feed off of it like they used to.

This story is not just another story; it is a parable of my life. You see, I was just like that lake. There have been many things I did that I did not include the Lord in. Praise the Lord that He is merciful. You see, I was overcome by weeds. I could no longer clean my lake out. All the equipment the Lord gave me was breaking down. I had no way to fix it because even though I never actually turned my back on Him I had gotten hard and would not let Him help me fix the equipment so that I could get rid of the weeds!

Thank God He sent me to Dunklin. Just like that lake, God sent in His people to clean out the weeds and show me how to keep my equipment in good shape.

The lake became beautiful and so have I. I am still here but people are able to see the beauty in me again and God is able to use me for His purpose. This is what discipleship is to me.

M.B. Saey

I would like to share with everyone what God has done for me. I was an alcoholic for 30 years – the older I grew, and the more money I made, the more alcohol I drank. My life was empty, worthless and miserable. I was at the end of my road when I heard about Dunklin Memorial Camp. I entered Dunklin on December 15, 1968. When I started to study the Bible I knew the only hope for me was Jesus Christ. Since I have been saved, I have a completely new life. I praise God for the freedom He has given me. *I now look for church steeples and crosses, instead of beer and liquor signs on the highway.*

EARL LETTELIER

I came to Dunklin Memorial Camp a little over three months ago for alcohol after this time period, I realize, that for me, this is not enough time. If I go through the program with the attitude of "serving time", or "counting the days", I harm myself. If I leave now, I am not ready spiritually, emotionally, or otherwise, to cope with any-thing once I leave the haven of the Camp. Three months, after years of alcoholism, is not enough for me. I realize it is only the beginning.

I am just now getting to the point of opening up in myself and my attitudes towards others. I am just starting to make progress, and I need further guidance and Bible study to solidly ground me to face whatever I have to cope with daily. The Lord has opened the way for me to be able to study in the Advanced Bible Class. This is to enable me to learn concepts of group leadership in the Laos ministry. This is the way for me to put the reality of Jesus ALIVE in my own life into action and to minister that faith and love to others through counseling and sharing.

No, dear brothers, I am still not all I should be, but I am bringing all my energies to bear on this one thing: forgetting the past and looking forward to what lies ahead. I strain to reach the end of what Christ Jesus did for me.

Jim Anderson

Since committing my life to Jesus, life is more exciting than I ever imagined. It has really helped Jim and me to rebuild our marriage, give my children a real family life, has helped me in my work, as well as my relationships with others. I am so thankful for the peace and joy Jesus brings to my heart.

There is only one way to live a happy and successful life. Without Jesus there is little happiness or meaning to life. I will forever be grateful to Brother Mickey for showing us how Jesus in His mercy can take two people in the depths of sin, wash away the dirt of sin and show us what truelove and beauty He has for us. How can we fail to forgive others when Jesus has forgiven us so much! I started drinking when I was 18 years old. I really thought I was something Back then, at 18, I knew all the answers (I thought). Little did I know of the pain and torment that lay ahead. I continued to drink for 22 years, each year putting me deeper and deeper into a hog pen.

At the age of 40, I had come "almost" to my wit's end. I had reached a time in my life when I didn't know which way to turn, or what to do. I had used all my resources; I had tried different ways to find relief from alcoholism, but nothing I tried worked.

I learned of D. M. C. through a good friend who brought me here. I had no idea what to expect, but at this stage I was ready to try anything. Actually, I had given up hope. I felt that life had ended for me, that I was doomed to a life of hell, all because of alcohol.

I could see Christ at work in other people but for almost six months, because of an inferiority complex and low self-image, I refused to turn loose of my own sell-will.

Finally I reached a point of desperation - this time I was at my wit's end. That's when it started to happen. I got down on my knees and for the first time, I prayed "honestly." I was a new man. Jesus came into my heart! I didn't fully understand what was happening, but I knew it was happening. But just a few days later, I left the camp and was gone three months. During that time I gradually returned to my old habits and attitudes and ended up going back to the bottle. After five days of drinking and pure hell, I knew I wanted no more of that life-style. I returned to the Camp, and found that God still wanted to pick me up and make me a part of His Kingdom. Praise God, all was forgiven and now I truly belong to Him.

Mack Underhill

After many years of drinkin more and more each year, I became a literal slave of alcohol. It was the number one thing in my life. I couldn't quit, even though I had been through the V.A. Hospital, State Alcoholic Rehabilitation Program and many other hospitals. My wife and family took it as long as they could, then they moved out. When my wife divorced me it was a shock but not enough to stop my drinking. Then in August 1966, I was persuaded to go to Dunklin Memorial Camp. Thank God my life hasn't been the same since then! I gained a whole new concept of who God is, His Word, and His way to live. I put my whole trust in Him and it's still there! My wife and I were remarried at the Camp and we have found a whole new way of life in Christ.

Jack Frost

My life was one not to be envied by anyone, except maybe the Devil, and as well he should have been proud of me, for I was one of his most faithful servants. I started drinking around the age of 17, and by 20 I was an old hand at it. I picked roughnecks who could drink the most, and swear the loudest as my role models.

I started out working steel during the summer and going to high school for the football season. When I wasn't eligible to play football anymore I quit school. I enjoyed structural steel work - anything high — smokestacks to skyscrapers, the higher the better. I thought I had reached the peak of life when I could drink and brawl all night, then go out and work on the high steel the next day. After years of this, I got married and started having children, but I still wanted to be a "Good Time Charlie" and the more I got drunk, the worse I would mistreat my family. I was always restless, always thinking that moving on to the next job would solve everything. I realize now that I was fighting God.

When I found myself at Dunklin, I didn't have any fight left in me. One Sunday night Jesus came into my life, and it literally felt as if a huge stone had been removed off my back. For the first time, I felt relaxed and at peace. At last I came face to face with the answer to all my restlessness and anxiety, as Jesus held his hand out to me.

Billy Lamb

I was an alcoholic. Drinking had been my life for ten years. I lost everything. After my divorce, I went home and lived with my parents. One night, in a drunken state, I woke up in jail. The judge told me that alcohol was making me act like a wildman. They were going to send me off to a mental institution, but decided to give me one more chance, if I would agree to go to this spiritual rehab for alcoholics.

I went to avoid the alternative, not for the purpose of coming to Christ. But when the grace of God appeared to me, I asked him to have mercy on my soul, and I surrendered my heart to Him. At that moment He began to mold me.

It's hard to write. How can a man explain an experience with Jesus Christ? Anyway, I now live a normal working life. I am remarried to my wife and we attend services at the Camp together. The damage whiskey did to my brain will probably never be restored, but the damage it has done to my heart has been more than restored.

He that cometh from above is above all and that includes whiskey!

Billy and Nadine Lamb.

"Hey, Melvin, got any money?"

"Not one nickel."

"Got anything to drink?"

"Not a drop. I quit."

"Yea, you quit .....who you kidding?"

Later on...the traffic light changes; the truck makes a swing to the left and comes up in the parking lot behind me. It is Sunday morning February 14, 1965 – Valentine's Day. Churches are already oper, but the bar 150 feet away won't be open until one o'clock. I'm waiting.

"Come over here," Melvin says to me.

"You want to some help?"

"More than anything in the world, Melvin."'

"Well then, get in and I'll get you some help."

Help to dirty, unshaven, wild-eyed me meant wine - the same wine that caused me to fall off my porch twice last night and left that row of scabs down my face.

"Okay, Melvin, let's get that help!"

"We'll go up to the hospital and see my wife. She has money."

A few minutes later Melvin comes out of the hospital with a cup of coffee and two aspirins which - I, thinking of the wine to come, dutifully swallow and say, "This ain't the way to the bar, Melvin."

"I know, but I haven't eaten lunch. Let's go to my house and eat."

So, to Melvin's home, where I, who had eaten one meal in the last two weeks - or was it three? - ate a toasted sandwich, a hot pastry and drank two glasses of cold milk. This would make a good base for the wine to come. I'm thinking Melvin should be good for a quart by now.

All this time Melvin has been droning on about some "Dunklin Camp" and somebody called Mickey. Now his wife who has just come in from work, joins in and even insists on reading about some guy named Al Cross from a paper called the "Campfire".

Seems this Al Cross found Jesus and is now staying sober and helping this Mickey.

"Al Cross?? Not the Al Cross I know ....

The bartender's pride? The tail end of the chain? Who has fallen off more bar stools than I ever sat on? Well, now, this I gotta see!

We get back in the truck. I'm intrigued by Al's apparent turnaround, but I still want that booze I've been waiting on all morning. We turn the corner, "Melvin, there are no bars on South 30th Street."

"I know, but I want to have a word with Sonny."

So the preacher, Sonny Holland comes out and joins the chorus ..... Dunklin Camp and Mickey .... ad nauseum.

"You need to go there now", says the preacher.

Apparently everyone is in agreement on this point but me. "I've got a lot of work to do. I'll go two weeks from today."

"Go now. Go now. Go now!"

"Okay, I'll go now."

Sonny says, "ok we'd better pray before you do."

This is how I was persuaded to go to Dunklin Memorial Camp for the six week program. Today lacks one day of being six weeks. As I sit here on this porch, I am fifteen pounds heavier, clean-shaven, clean in body, mind and soul. I kneeled in the straw at the altar with Mickey four weeks ago tonight and accepted Jesus as my personal Savior.

I have no money, no worries, no cares and no doubts. I am going back to my family, and I hope to bring them and many others to the same Jesus that changed me.

Mr. Merrill, Thurman Deskins and Mickey planting peach trees donated by Aunt Susie Sigmond.

John Thomas

I came from Tampa to the wilderness of Dunklin on the night of 26 September, 1970. Pouring down rain, eighteen miles from the nearest bar with lots of snakes between if I chose to leave (I was told). There were no phones. Communication with the outside world was by mail, car or plane.

Rev. Bob Shelley introduced me to Bro. Mickey and promptly left. I was taken to the drunk tank for my abode. Then I wandered down to the old mess hall where a Good Samaritan meeting was going on. I learned right away I could not smoke inside with my coffee. Neither could I take coffee outside with my cigarette. So I took leave of Good Sam and went back to my drunk tank to smoke and sulk outside in the rain with shakes and regrets. What am I in for now? I kept wondering.

Two days later I met with Bro Mickey in his office and he asked me why I had come to DMC. I told him to be reunited with God. That was my favorite snow-job for preachers. He stated right back, "John, I don't believe you've ever been united with God in the first place. How can you reunite with someone you've never known?'

I found salvation, and that was the beginning of my recovery ... physically, mentally and spiritually.

The DMC property west of the barn was all swamp and cabbage palms, but this was about to change. Bro. Mickey put me and Jack Phipps out there one day and said, "Don't look at all the roots and mud you're wading knee-deep in, boys. Look ahead to the lovely orange trees and buildings that will be here." When he left Jack and I said he was crazy! We named that part of the camp the Root Patch.

Two months later Tommy Underhill and I went to Indiantown with Bro. Mickey to purchase barbed wire. On the way back along Fox Brown Road Bro. Mickey pointed out five miles of fence and said, "This is the barbed wire I bought."

We almost choked! For three weeks Tommy and I took down five strands of barbed wire and fence posts and then planted and strung the same around the airstrip and the Root Patch.

The Root Patch is now (twenty years later) orange grove, an office building and two multi-level living quarters.

I learned that Bro. Mickey wore many hats. He taught our Bible study classes starting at 7:30am. Then he changed to his work clothes or cowboy outfit for camp labor or cow work. Then he changed to a suit and tie to preach or to his butcher clothes to butcher a beef or hog for chow….. and then changed to interview a new man. Or in between these duties he might be off into the wild blue yonder in his Cessna to preach a revival.

At this point Bro. Mickey had only a student pilot license and could not take passengers up. When he learned I had a commercial pilot's rating with instrument, he took me along. I hung my license on the windshield of the Cessna, and Bro. Mickey flew her. I got some mighty good counseling on those flights which has been invaluable to this day.

As part of our advanced Bible class, Bro. Mickey took us to witness to the alcoholics in the farm fields of Immokalee.

Bible School Men on 2 Day Trip
To Immokalee

The greatest event that happened to me at DMC (except for my salvation) was that my wife and I were remarried in the Tabernacle by Bro. Mickey on 20 December, 1970 with Laura Maye playing the piano and all the Camp family in attendance. This was the greatest of salvation gifts having wife returned to me.

Forty years later, John's grandson came through the program .

Frosty Bennett

On December 22, 1967, after one snort too many, God directed the front end of my car into the rear end of the car in front of me as we were stopping for a traffic light. My life, already a mess, just got worse. For the past sixty years I had lived a life of spiritual stagnation, and was about as useful to the Lord as a bucket of beer.

In January, Jake Magenhiemer, who was a personal friend of Bro. Mickey, drove me to Dunklin. I shall never forget my introduction to Mickey. He's a big fellow, and the very sight of him nearly scared the life out of me - until I literally *saw* the compassionate love of Jesus Christ in his eyes.

There was nothing impersonal about our first encounter. He looked me straight in the eyes and asked. "Mr. Bennett, are you a Christian?" After a moment of reflection, I assured him I was. Then came a hard left to the jaw. "What makes you think you can do the things you have been doing to propel you to the Camp and still be a Christian?"

My life up to that point had been like that of so many others that call themselves Christians, but have never really made Christ their Lord. I went to Sunday School, was baptized at 14, and was a fairly-regular church-goer. My preacher would describe my type of Christianity as "the ordinary garden variety with a lot of weeds in it."

I decided I'd better keep my mouth shut until we got better acquainted. After a little more sparring around he agreed to let me stay if I would agree to stick with the program. It would be a tough two months though, and he was going to proceed to kill the "old man" Bennett to make way for the birth of a new one.

The first thing "we" (meaning he) were going to do was get rid of my foolish pride. What a statement to make! Why, everyone in Miami knew that I was the most humble man in Florida, and here was this young 37 year old preacher accusing me, a mature man of 60, of being prideful? Presumptuous insolence, that's what it was!

Here I am in the midst of the Everglades, miles from the nearest town. No mail service. No telephone. Only the owls to hoot me to sleep at night and a noisy peacock to wake me in the morning.

The center of activity is in the Tabernacle. It is a large church built by men such as myself while they were going through the program, and it is here that Bible Study and church services are held every day. It is here too, that one night I hit the dust on my knees, and a new babe in Christ was born.

Florida Indians singing about Jesus in the old, straw-floored tabernacle.

Friday night is the big night at the Camp. People from around the countryside gather in boots and shirtsleeves to pray, sing and worship. Any man caught wearing a necktie is obligated to sing a solo or drop ten dollars in the offering bucket.

Bro. Mickey (always tieless, except for that one occasion that started the joke) raises his arms and eyes to Heaven and sings, *Oh, How I love Jesus* until I'm sure the cows in the far corner of the northwest forty have shivers running up and down their spines.

There is no set closing hour. They just sing and pray until the Holy Spirit tells them it is time to go home. No service concludes, however, without an altar call. It was on such a Friday night, January 12, 1968, that I went forward, got on my knees and turned over to the Lord whatever was left of my life.

I had finally realized what it meant to accept Christ's invitation when he said "Behold, I stand at the door and knock; if any man hear My voice and open the door I will come in to him and sup with him and he with me."

At some point in my life I may have opened the door to him, but then just left Him standing outside, without inviting Him in to "sup with me and I with Him". I locked the door back and He had never been permitted inside my heart. I stood rebelliously on the other side holding the key in my pocket. That night, I re-opened that door and this time I handed Him the key. I don't ever want it back.

My wife and teenage children visited me at Dunklin, and the Holy Spirit seized my younger daughter's heart. She is now one of the most active members in Youth for Christ in our community.

After completing the program I returned to Miami to straighten out my legal problems. God sent me to a young Christian lawyer who, at my trial, introduced a brochure of the Camp as evidence of what God is doing for men such as me. The judge agreed my problem was solved. A few months later, my driver's license was restored, a job came to me, providing twice the salary I was making before I resigned to go to Dunklin, and I am spending my money more wisely.

My young Christian lawyer met my older daughter, and on their first date took her to church and she got saved. Now our family is finally complete in the faith.

We visit the Camp often to hear the excellent preachers like Bob Mumford, Peter Lord and the teachers who come and hold marriage retreats for the men in the program and their families which they also open up to the churches in the surrounding communities.

Frosty and Family

Mickey: Another tradition we can usually count on each Homecoming, is a visit by Mel-Paul. We first became acquainted with Melvin as he was known then, when

as a teenager he would accompany his parents, Mr. and Mrs. Aldredge out to the Camp for the Friday night sings each weekend. They were great believers in the work the Lord was doing at Dunklin.

Even though a shy teenager, Melvin had experienced a powerful deliverance from drugs and was on fire for the Lord and had a heart for the lost. We gladly sponsored him on a missions trip to Guatemala and when he got back he was even more fired up and certain of the Lord's call on his life to be a missionary.

Shortly afterwards, Mel was in a serious motorcycle accident. It left him paralyzed and in a coma. Upon his parents request I flew to Vero Beach to pray for him. Vernon Wright, a friend whom I had grown up with in Okeechobee, was now the chaplain at the Indian River Jail. He arranged to pick me up at the airport and went with me to see Melvin.

It had been a few days since the accident with no signs of recovery. The prognosis was that he would remain in a vegetative state. We circled around the bed with his parents, laid hands on him and began to pray. While we were praying, Melvin opened up his eyes. As we began to rejoice and continued praying, slowly he started to speak. *He literally came back to life before our very eyes!*

As we left the room, we were praising the Lord and "walking on cloud nine". I think I could have flown all the way home without the airplane!

God used the accident in Melvin's life like the experience Paul had on the Damascus Road. He emerged from the coma, no longer shy, but now very bold in his witness for Christ, and what He had done in his life. So like the apostle, proclaiming the Gospel with passion and boldness, he become known as Mel-Paul.

His zeal for winning the lost has never dimmed. He has traveled the country much like Paul with no house of his own, working with his hands for room and board along the way, to wherever the Lord calls him next.

Every year we look forward to welcoming him home to Dunklin and Homecoming is just not the same when he can't be here. You'll know him if you see him. He'll be the one with the big smile picking up palm fronds and singing Jesus Loves Me.

To this very hour we go hungry and thirsty, we are in rags, we are brutally treated, we are homeless. We work hard with our own hands. When we are cursed, we bless; when we are persecuted, we endure it; when we are slandered, we answer kindly.

1 Corinthians 4:11-13

Melvin Arledge in his own words before the accident.

On Sunday, November 30, 1975, my miserable, frustrated, dirty, drug-filled life was ended, and my eyes were opened to the Truth. The light of Jesus filled my soul. I finally found out who I was, why I am here on earth and the assurance I have that I'm going to heaven when my course here on earth is finished.

I stayed at Dunklin for eight months, learning about dealing with my problems and renewing my mind. I was under the constant care of Jesus. It was rough sometimes, but I found that there is no change without pain.

Then, through prayer, I found God's will for the summer, when God sent me to Guatemala to rebuild buildings for the churches – using His children here at Dunklin to support me.

Once there, the incredible summer began as God was pouring His love and Holy Spirit on the Team - unifying us.

We were constantly aware of God's hand on us, delivering us from sickness and the devil. We, with God's love, touched the natives and made them aware of God's love and the fact that God answered their prayers for new buildings.

We took the gospel of Jesus to many in need and gave many testimonies. God richly blessed me in knowledge and filled me with His Holy Spirit. And, I am still under His extreme care, growing as a child of God.

I never believed being saved was so wonderful, even with its valleys. So, praise His name! His will be done forever in me on earth and in heaven.

"Que Dios le bendiga." May God bless you!

In Christ's Most Abundant Love, Melvin

DYING WITH HONOR

Cary E. Hanna was on heroin when he came to the Camp in 1969 from New York. He was the first drug addict to come through the program. He did well, and responded to God's call on his life. Later on, he went to a Christian and Missionary Alliance College in Toccoa, Georgia to advance his training for ministry.

Above the campus, a fifty-five acre lake was held in place by an old earthen embankment built in 1887. Below the dam, Toccoa Creek plunged 186 feet in an uninterrupted drop, to emerge from a canyon beside the school.

On November 5, 1977 heavy rains weakened the dam. In the wee hours of the morning, the dam broke. Within minutes, a wall of water, traveling 120 miles an hour, smashed into the campus killing thirty-nine people.

Cary was able to get out of the water, but he went back in to try to help somebody else, and they both drowned.

His father asked if Cary could be buried at Dunklin. He

was the first person buried here. His memorial stone faces east, overlooking Lake Elijah.

Danny Ray Owens

By the time I was 11-12 yrs old, I was a full blown alcoholic. I worked and drank on the dairies just like a grown man. My earthly father was the only one that could control me because I was so scared of him.

1974 was my first time going through the program at Dunklin; I had just turned 16 yrs old. I was the first teen to go through the program. I knew about Dunklin from my Daddy going to Dunklin a couple of years before I got there. In 1973, my Daddy passed and my wild days started. When I got to the Camp in 1974, Preacher Mickey took me under his wing and tried to show me the way of the Lord. I didn't go to the Camp because I wanted to; I went to stay out of jail. When I was in the program the first time there were only 10-12 men in it with me. In those days a young man was 30+ yrs old, I changed that rule with thanks to the Preacher. I learned a lot from all the good men and staff members, Mickey & Laura Maye did a little bit of everything, Mickey was the Preacher, the teacher & the candle stick maker. He sure had his hands full with trying to teach all us hard headed drunks as to why we should give our life to the Lord instead of the bottle. It worked with me and I was saved and baptized that same year. In those days the program was 8 weeks long for a married man, 12 weeks for a single man but when Mickey got a hold of me I had to stay for 6 months! I actually stayed about a year. Even though the next 40 years had its ups and downs, the people I met and things I learned always had a big influence on my life. I had the good fortune of knowing Mickey & Laura Maye and the kids who became like my brothers & sisters. Preacher Mickey is still "Dad" to me. Mickey and the "family" were there at one of my darkest periods, when my first wife passed and they were there at one of the brightest times, when Mickey married me to my second wife. Over the course of the next 40 years I repeated the program a few times and I always learned something new, about myself, life and my walk with the Lord. Dad still doesn't know what to think about me sometimes, I would call him at all hours of the night, drunk and sober and he never gave up on me, always would talk to me and pray for me. I always knew I could count on Mickey to put in a good word for me with the Lord and together they would bring me threw the rough times. I still say the Preacher is holding Gods hands.

One example of Preacher Mickey's teachings, when I first started at the camp I was not a very good reader or speller so I would have to recite the verses to the Preacher, I learned them well! Recently I had to have two surgeries on my head, (due to a brain bleed) I didn't know a person around me and from what I was told when I did talk, it often made no sense. But when my sister asked me about the verse John 3:16, I was able to tell her! And then slowly I began to recite other scriptures. The Lord promised that He would bury His Word in our hearts, and that proved true. The Dunklin Program has always been a stabilizing force in my life. I can attest to having seen many miracles happen in my life.

Myself being one of them, when I had my brain bleed and surgery in April the Doctors told my wife to call my sister to come right away and those same Doctors repeatedly telling my wife and sister it would be a long recovery if I recovered at all. But I'm still here, must be the Lord still has something for me to do.

Mickey: I first met Danny Owens in the Okeechobee jail. He was fourteen years old and had been arrested along with his Daddy for stealing calves from the dairy they worked on to sell for whiskey. They were both alcoholics. The foreman had mercy on them and didn't want to press charges, he just wanted to see them get some help, so he called me. Danny's father came in to the program shortly after that and

The first time Danny came in the program, he walked into my office and I could hear him sloshing. I pulled his pants leg up and he had a quart of liquor tucked in his boot. He took off running and went and hid in the woods for about an hour, then he finally came back in and handed me the bottle.

Norman Hales had given us 50 head of dairy calves to raise and Danny's father took care of them.

   Danny may hold the record for times in the program. At least four. He's also served on our staff. When he is sober, he is a very good man – a very hard worker.

"He has made us able ministers of the new covenant—
not of the letter but of the Spirit; for the letter kills,
but the Spirit gives life."
II Corinthians 3:6

The Strongitharms were a living example of this verse.

We welcome Bro. Gordon and Bernice Strongitharm back into our fellowship once again. They have served the Lord faithfully on the mission field in Brazil for ten years with the New Tribes Mission.

Chapter 16:
Pilots, Police Officers, Convicts and Cowboys
...and some who were all four!

Layman's Landing, a lay outreach, was started by a group of men including Reid Hardin, Gordon Sparks and Wayne Cole who were pilots, loved to fly, loved the Lord and would go anywhere, anytime, to tell others what Christ had done in their lives. We got together and had fly-ins to prisons all over the state for teaching sessions.

Layman's Landing Team

Several pilots involved in the Layman's Landing joined me flying up to the Florida State Prison for weekend retreats. We stayed in the officer's quarters and went from cell to cell on Death Row, held services in the chapel and ministered to the men. We took the young men from Dunklin who were in Servant Leadership Training to give them experience in prison ministry. Our philosophy is that if you are a Christian, you're also a minister.

Many of our men had the privilege of participating in

weekend missions with the Layman's Landing teams, and they shared their testimonies all over the state. It gave our men the added opportunity of close fellowship with the dedicated Christians who were involved in the Lay Witness movement. Some of these same men are still reaching out to prisoners all over the world, because Layman's Landing pilots took time to encourage them and equip them for the work of ministry.

Chaplain Max Jones had been transferred up from Belle Glade the Florida State Prison in Starke where Austin ended up as a chaplain as well. We landed on the runway and taxied right up to the fence surrounding the prison. Max walked out, opened the gate for us, and gave me a big hug.

FINDING FREEDOM behind bars are former Martin County sheriff's deputies John Roberts, left, and Gerald Brown right. Sentenced to prison in 1976 for dealing in marijuana, they are attending classes at Dunklin Memorial Camp with their prison chaplain, Warren B. Wall, right center. Dunklin, a haven of hope for the down and out, is the realization of a dream of the Rev. Mickey Evans, left center. Photo by Richard L. Myers

Jack Murphy, the infamous jewel thief, was in lock-up on the Q Wing, He told me later that he was standing at the window when we landed. When he saw Max walk out to meet me, he said to himself, "I wish I had a friend like that to hug me."

That weekend he got saved.

John Roberts and Gerald Brown were some local good ole boys among the inmates whose wives Theresa and Joanne, joined them for the marriage retreats, and then became some of the first prison ministers trained at Dunklin. They had been our personal friends, and worked as sheriff's deputies in Indiantown.

They got tangled up in a conspiracy to sell confiscated drugs, and were sentenced to prison.

After serving their time, their testimony had double strength, because they had been on both sides of the law and God had gotten ahold of their hearts and set them on fire for Him.

"I had the pleasure of attending the first Inmate Training School at Dunklin and it changed my Christian life by teaching me how to love my fellow man. It changed my life and our prison. I never had so much peace in my life; my wife and I are in love for the first time and are having a great time in prison watching the Lord work. God has finally got it through my head that prison is where He wants me for now so I can be happy in prison and the school helped me over that wall that I had put up. I've become more bold in my witness for Christ and I thank God for it."   ~ Gerald Brown

Frank Costantino

I met Frank Constantino when he was serving time in Belle Glade Prison. He had been a dangerous career criminal, head of the Miami Mob.   One day Max asked me to teach a marriage class for prisoners with wives. I asked him if there was any possibility they would release the men to come to the Camp, so the wives could meet them in a better environment. I don't know how he did it, but Max got the warden to release them, and he brought them out in a bus. Their wives met them here, and Laura Maye and I started The Family Recovery Classes. Frank and his wife, Bunny, were one of the first couples in our class. Frank and Bunny began growing in the Lord and started their own prison ministry called Bridges Over America and he which "wrote the book" on aftercare and provided halfway houses for men coming out of prison. They developed cutting edge curriculum and their ministry has had an international impact.

Madonna, Laura Mae, Melissa, Skip and Ginny

Another sherriff's deputy named Skip Bryant and his wife Ginny served faithfully on our staff. Skip was tragically killed while flying a search and rescue mission over Lake Okeechobee. He is still fondly remembered by all who knew him. Ginny has continued to serve the Lord and bless others with her beautiful singing voice and all three daughters have grown into lovely young ladies.

AUSTIN'S TESTIMONY

"God rescued me from the grave,
and now my life is filled with light."
Job 33:28

We'd all been drinking. We were all drunk! One of the guys came at me with a knife - and then another guy too. I pulled out a gun and started shooting. I wasn't exactly shooting at him; there were two of them. I was just shooting.

Then I ran. I got outta there. I sure wasn't going back and check that out. I got outta there and went about my business. I didn't know I had hit anybody.
That was April 14, 1962 in Pompano Beach, Florida.

Better than a year later they caught me in Miami at the International Airport driving my uncle's car, drunk with no driver's license. A state trooper picked me up and wanted to know where I was going. I didn't know. No place. So he took me to jail and charged me with driving without a license.

I could have gotten out if I could raise $25, but I couldn't even round up $25 anywhere. I stayed in jail two or three days. Then they realized that Broward County had an arrest warrant out for me … for murder.

They came down and questioned me, and I didn't even try to deny it. I was tired of the whole thing. I was thirty-four years old, had a drunk and disorderly and petty larceny arrest record which stretched back almost twenty years. Now I had killed a man. I was tired of the whole thing. I was just tired.

A couple months later I was serving a fifteen-year sentence for manslaughter at Glades Correctional Institution (GCI) in Belle Glade, Florida.

I got saved out on a ditch bank hoeing weeds. Me and seventeen other convicts were out there clearing up ditches at a farm camp. It was hot and I was miserable as I could be. All those younger convicts were complaining about everything, and it just wore me out. I was the oldest guy out there.

I worked up and got away from them, and God started working with me. He said, "Hey, you're thirty-eight years old. You've got nothing to show for your life. The clothes you have on are not even yours." I started crying and saying I was sorry. "You're right, Lord. I'm sorry!" Then it was like all those years seemed to wash off me. I felt happy and free for the first time.

I started working faster. The guy who was boss said, "Austin, what's the matter with you?"

"Nothing. I'm all right. I'm all right," I said. I couldn't wait to get in that evening and tell Max Jones, our Chaplain, about it. When I did go see him I didn't even get the words out of my mouth. He took one look at me and laughed and said, "Tell me what happened." When I told him he said, "You're saved!"

I didn't know anything about God or religion. I'd never had a Bible in my whole life, but for the next four years the Bible was food to me. After the first two years Max started me teaching a Bible class. I didn't know anything about teaching a class, but it made me study. Max gave me three or four guys and told me to go at it.

Inmates have a strong trust and respect for other inmates when they see them not playing games. You can't fool convicts, because they are the most cynical people in the world, and if it isn't the real thing they'll let you know.

All I know is I had a hunger for the Lord and His word, and I wanted to share it with them. That's all. I lived that way for the next two years and just grew. It was wonderful. Mickey started coming out there and holding services. Then Max started taking some of us to Dunklin Camp to the Tent Meetings.

So we would go out and spend the whole day, enjoy the Fish Fry and have a Gospel Sing - fifteen or twenty of us. That place would be packed with people. That used to be something.

When so much has gone wrong in your life, you want to distance yourself from people, because you don't think they'll accept you anyway. It makes a loner out of you.

Coming out here to Dunklin was special. By then I was a Christian, but I had never experienced the love I felt at Dunklin. We need somebody to accept us - not just to tolerate us, but God's people are the only people who can do that. I needed somebody on the outside to help me grow, and Mickey was it - and this Camp. The Holy Spirit is so strong out at Dunklin. Hcooo-eee! When you walk out there, you know it's holy ground.

Carl Langley, a white man, had served thirty-five years in prison, and he came to Belle Glade one Sunday night to give his testimony. I was sitting up there listening, and the

Lord put it in my heart. I said, "Lord when I get out of prison that's what I want to do. I want to come back and let these men know what you've done in my life."

That was two and a half years before I got out.
Bob Lee, the personnel manager at the Glades Coop Sugar Mill, used to bring his ukulele to the prison and sing with us. One day I was working for the superintendent - walking that dog on a leash. Bob said to me, "Austin, you've got a job when you get out of prison." God worked that out two years before I got released. I didn't have to worry about getting out and finding a job.

Oct 28, 1968 when I was released from prison. The very next night after my release I was back in Belle Glade Prison ……. teaching a Bible class. I went straight to see Bob, and he took me under his wing. I worked at the sugar mill till 1974 when I went up to the State Prison.

When God saves you He doesn't turn you loose to do your own thing. He trains you He trains in three sections. First He trained me thirty-eight years by allowing things to happen in my life to train me for the people he wanted me to minister to. After I got saved he had to start another training, teaching me how to be obedient to work out His plan.

Then God put me on a leash and let me make failure after failure until after awhile I wanted to do it His way. We're all in a hurry. He wants us to relax and let Him work it out - not us.

As soon as I got out of prison I came out to Dunklin all the time. I couldn't wait to get off work on the weekends. By that time Mickey was taking me places with him. He'd go to preach and he took me to give my testimony.

We'd fly in his plane, and we had some fun too. One time Mickey told me to meet him over in Belle Glade to fly somewhere. That joker got me in the plane and flew right over the prison. You just don't do that.

They got those towers up there with guns. Someone might fly in and take convicts out. It's against the law! Anyway he got over the prison and turned loose that steering thing and said, "All right. You got it!" I didn't know he could steer that plane with his feet. I thought he meant it. I grabbed the wheel and almost wrecked the both of us. I think I scared him as much as me!

Sometimes I flew with him up to Stark to the state prison. He would preach and teach in small groups. He loves small groups. Mickey was the finest Bible teacher. It was a good time.

One night a lady I knew at Dunklin came up to me and said, "Brother Austin, I have someone I want you to meet," and she gave me a phone number. People did that a lot, because I was traveling with Adrian Rogers, David Smith and Mickey and meeting a lot of people at that time. I stuck the note in my pocket and didn't think much about it. About a week later the Holy Spirit spoke to me about that little phone number.

I started trying to find it. When I finally found it, I called. The voice on the other end belonged to a Miss Jeanette Smith. She said she was going to North Carolina to visit family, but when she returned we could meet up if I'd like. I had been out of prison a while and just loved the Lord. I didn't think I needed a family to tie me down. So, I wasn't really looking for a wife. Maybe we could just be friends.

When Jeanette came back I went over and we talked. We drove out to Dunklin one night to a service. And God told me - just like I'm speaking to you now - "That's your wife." That's all he said, "That's your wife."

We were down in the Chow Hall. We stepped out that side door, and I said, "The Lord told me that you are going to be my wife."

She looked at me and said, "What are you saying? Are you asking me to marry you or something?" "Yes. The Lord told me that, so I'm asking you," I said.

She loved the Lord too, and He had been speaking to her heart. So we had a short engagement and got married in the Tabernacle here at Dunklin Memorial Camp. And it was packed! Everybody wanted to see us get married! The people at Dunklin gave us a big wedding. All we had to do was show up. God didn't want us to have a dead wedding either… with the death march and all that. I had six groomsmen, and only one was African American like me. The rest were all white guys who had gone through the program at Dunklin and got saved. We sang two songs. My wife's song was *Blessed Assurance*. Then every man got up and gave a testimony about how the Lord had saved him. We were married, and as we were marching out I sang *I'll Fly Away.* It was something!

When Jennie and I married she had a daughter, Jawanda, by a previous marriage, so I adopted her. I don't believe in this step-daddy stuff. I had been told when I went in the Navy and again when I went in prison that, due to an illness I had as a child, I was sterile and would have no children. The Lord healed my body, and Jeanette and I have four daughters. Jawanda works in journalism. Austine is Captain in the Marine Corp. Janelle is an anesthesiologist. My baby, Rosa Lee is a lawyer. I thank God for each one.

Jeanette was a school teacher. She worked for the state in the educational system, and they transferred her from Palm Beach up to Gainesville.

I stayed down here a couple months getting miserable. I was praying about what to do. Then I got a phone call from Chaplain Max Jones. He had been transferred from Glades Correctional up to Florida State Prison in Stark. That's only twenty-five miles from Gainesville. He said, "Hey, Bud. How would you like to stop making all that money and come up here and starve with me some?"

I said, "What do you mean, Max?"

He said, "The warden wants you up here." I like to of went through the ceiling! That answered everything. "Lord, this is what you had for me all along!" I said.

I resigned my job at the sugar mill, and headed for Stark. From the time I walked into that prison I loved it. I tell people the most miserable person in the world is a preacher who doesn't feel the call of God in his life, and he's somewhere trying to make it work. I knew God was in it, because He brings contentment.

I'd be eternally grateful no matter where or how I got saved. But as it is, I'm just a little extra thankful that I was saved in jail. Because that makes me a natural for the jail ministry. I'm glad of that because nothing "turns me on" like the opportunity to share with a bunch of guys what the Lord did for me while I was "building time." Sometimes, at the beginning, the men show little interest; but when they hear that I've been there too, they begin to tune in – especially when they hear me thank God for every day I was locked up. Some men think I've flipped when they hear this. But I thank the Lord because then I can tell them what I know for sure – that there is solid hope and sure help - no matter what the problem. Jesus said, "Come to me, all ye that labor and are heavy laden, and will give you rest." And He says, "and him that cometh to me I will in no way cast out." Thank God, I know He means what He says because He did this for me while I was behind bars. I was really "heavy laden" - loaded down. But the moment I cried out in earnest He heard me, and answered me, and calmed my heart, and gave me rest – and I've never been the same since. I praise Him and thank Him for His mercy and His goodness.

You have to earn the trust of men in prison. I worked with the death row men. That cell is his home, and even though I was a Chaplain, I respected that. When I went back there talking to them I'd say, "Hey, Pete. How you doin'? You wanna talk a little bit?"

He may say "I'm kinda up tight. Give me some slack." "O.k., I'll see you some other time." And I'd leave.

You get their permission to talk. They aren't going anywhere. We have to earn their respect. That is what we miss in Christianity. We try to throw something at people. Sometimes they have more manners than we have. If I force a conversation on them, they might be polite enough not to rag me out about it, but they're thinking, "Where's this guy coming from!"

When I go back there I don't take any power either. We drink coffee. We talk about baseball. We talk about his family. I want him talking. He might talk about anything he wants to, and we might not bring up the name of the Lord. I earn that right for us to talk and I let God do His job. The Holy Spirit is the one who sets these things up - not me.

I had Ted Bundy fourteen years. I know what he did, but it was none of my business. For the thirty years I worked there I never looked in a man's file to find out what he did. I'm a human being, and I can't look at all that negativity and not be affected by it. It would affect me. I put their judgment in God's hands.

People think the men on Death Row would accept the Lord more readily, but that's not so. People don't get saved out of fear. We get saved because of the love of God.

Scripture says, *But where sin abounded, grace did much more abound.*

Romans 5:20

We also used those old tents for Cowboy Campmeetings at rodeos. Just before a rodeo, we would set up the tent and hold services. Many cowboys who had never darkened the door of a church building, rode their horses right up to that rickety tent and ended up surrendering their hearts to the Lord.

After the last tent blew away, The Clemons family let us hold cowboy revivals at the Okeechobee Livestock Market. We would even lower Laura Maye's piano right down into the auction pit. I bet old "Liberace" never got to play *his* piano in such as classy joint!

Okeechobee Livestock Market

Testimony of
Leon Myers

On September 17, 1977, I had an experience that changed my whole life. I met Jesus  Christ at the Okeechobee Livestock Market. He put me on my knees and I had to stay there a while.

Being a cowboy and trying to live up to what a cowboy is supposed to be (rough, tough and not humbling himself to anyone) God had his work cut out. For many years, I had "done it my way" no matter who it hurt. But thanks to God and His Son, Jesus Christ, I've learned to love and be loved. Christ is teaching me to love and really have an understanding of what love is. He is teaching me obedience and showing me great things through prayer. He has given me patience to cope with my daily problems and such a peace and a joy in my heart. I just want to share this joy with everyone.

John Murphy: On October 28, 1977, at Dunklin Memorial Camp, I had an experience and now I am able to let down the fence I had built around myself. Prior to that time, I felt like I had wasted 37 years of my life. I could never find satisfaction in my work and personal life. It got so that my burden was too heavy to bear. It was then that I humbled myself and asked Christ to come into my life and He did. Since then, it has been so much better. I am able to cope with problems that arise as a law enforcement officer, and in my personal life. I have found a love for my fellowman that I never knew existed before.

Bill Sherman

What is happiness? Is it having enough money to last a lifetime and your children's? Is it respectability from mankind for who you are and what you have done? For forty years of my life, I thought happiness was to be found in those things, but I was wrong, dead wrong.

Happiness is to be found in one person – JESUS.

I achieved a measure of financial success in the eyes of the world, held public offices and owned things I thought would make me happy. But I wasn't, I was miserable and riddled with anxiety. After I had tried everything else, I finally turned to the Lord. In Psalms 51:12, David asks the Lord to "restore unto me the joy of thy salvation". I know what David was talking about. I have committed myself to the Jesus and He has replaced my anxiety with peace and joy. I thank and praise Him for all He has done for me. I don't have the words to describe the difference Jesus has made in my life. I now have the ability to love my fellow man. I really care about people, and He has helped me understand what this life is all about, why I am here, and where I am going. The Bible is easier to understand and therefore is a comfort to me and also a guide for my everyday life. What the Lord has done for me, He will do for you too if you just let Him.

Mack and Sharon Roberts

 I grew up in the church, joined when I was about 10, and even after marriage, we attended church fairly regularly, but I wasn't really concerned about spiritual matters. Over a period of 16 years, I made a few shallow commitments to God. In March of 1975, I attended a Cowboy Camp Meeting and was convicted of my sins against God and made sure that if I hadn't been saved before, I wanted to now. The devil tried to convince me that I had gone too far, That the Lord would have none of me. But from that night , I asked the Lord to really come into my life and make a new person out of me. I know that He did, for I have been a new person ever since. Jesus said that the devil is a liar and the truth is not in him. He also said "I am come that ye might have life and have it more abundantly." I am learned daily to depend upon Jesus more and more, for He is the door to the Father. I study the Word every day, for faith comes by hearing the Word. I love Jesus. He has saved my soul and He is my Lord. Praise His Name!

Eddie Mattson

I was saved when I was 11 years old. I went to church and worked at being a Christian a little, not much. If you don't really get in there and kick that self-will out and let the Holy Spirit in, you just not going to get far with the Lord – and I didn't!

When I got older, I got involved with running horses at the track, started injecting myself with the same drugs we used to dope up the horses, and became addicted to them. It got to where I would "shoot up" 15-20 times a day!

In salvation, I think a lot of us try to give 50% of ourselves to the Lord and hold back 50% for ourselves. We have to give Him a 100%, that's what I have learned from my life. When I finally realized that I had become a real bona fide drug addict, I tried hard to kick the habit on my own, but I wouldn't let the Lord help me, I thought "He didn't get me in this mess, so it's up to me to get myself out of it."

Eventually, my wife had enough and divorced me. I responded by diving even deeper into my addiction. Before long, I became really depressed and gave up on life. I didn't care about anything or anybody, anymore. My body had taken about all it could – I'd shot up everything they make and I tried to end my life five times during this period.

Thankfully, I ended up in jail. Mickey came to visit me and offered to take me into the program, but when he realized what a bad attitude I still had, he didn't think there was much chance of me making it through it and told me so. So I sat in jail for a while longer.

When my Dad bailed me out, I decided to go to Dunklin anyway and "try it out". I was there for two weeks and not really getting anything out of it. So, I took off, just about a week before my sentencing. Two encounters I had convinced me to go back to DMC and finish up those last five days. Before my sentencing I prayed most of the night and asked Bro. Mickey if he would let me come back if the judge agreed. He asked why I wanted to come back and I sincerely told him I needed it for myself. That was the answer he was looking for, and it was a turning point in my life. The judge let me go back to Dunklin. Four weeks later, I was still searching, looking for something - I wasn't sure just what – but knew I wasn't finding it here.

Then one evening as I was doing my homework, something just started happening. I got down on my knees and God met me right there and the Holy Spirit came down. I said "Lord, now I know what the problem is. I've been trying to give You a little of my life and keep the rest for me, dishing it out however it suited old me. I see it right now. I need to give everything to You and just let You lead me in whatever You want me to do."

Things started changing. I began witnessing and going to the prisons to share what the Lord was doing for me. It's really been beautiful what's happened in my life.

Matty Spinelli

For 22 years, I didn't go to church. My wife had Christ in her heart, but I didn't allow her the privilege of taking our children to church. I had lost my hand as a young man. After this happened, I happened, I went outside and looked up to Heaven and cursed God. I had been strong and thought my sunburned neck and calloused hand were the only thing that achieved my way of life, the way I made a living. I'd become quite good at horseshoeing and I thought I had done it all on my own. One day I got tired of Long Island where I was from and decided to move to Florida. I found some property in Okeechobee and met Eddie Matson. I didn't know why then but I know now that the Lord brought me all the way from New York to Okeechobee to meet Eddie who took me to Dunklin where I met Jesus and was reborn. Shortly after the Lord began working in my life, but I didn't understand what He was doing. The Lord actually started to prepare me for my son's death several months before it happened. Through the circumstances He was using I got very upset and went to Bro. Mickey. I told him I didn't know how to pray about this situation. He guided me to Matthew 5 where it says if you ask God, He will give you what you need.

I tried to pray but no answer came and finally I got so mad at my wife for trying to figure out what was bugging me, I quit going to church again and told her I was through with this whole God business! Actually, I was ashamed because, I didn't understand the Lord was preparing me for what was to come, and I was afraid to talk about it. Later that same week, my wife called me at work and told me our son had been shot to death. On the plane trip to Long Island for the funeral, I asked God to forgive me for not realizing what He was doing and becoming so angry with Him and everyone else. Soon, I was able to pray for my wife who was heart-broken and sick over losing our son. The Lord immediately answered and we realized His love and grace in a much deeper way through this experience. I just thank and praise the Lord that He is in my heart and soul and is at work every day in my life.

Wendell Cooper

On February 4, I will be one year old in the Lord, which really makes me a baby Christian. I praise God for sending His Son to pay for all my sins and save a guy like me.

For 17 years I made the mistake of thinking money and happiness go together. My whole life was geared to making money and I was confident that if I could only get rich that all my problems would disappear. Being a working cowboy, I finally realized I had two chances of getting rich---slim and none. But had another goal in life that I felt there was a chance to attain, and that was to be a champion in the sport of rodeo . Steer wrestling was my favorite event and I was determined to be the champion of Florida. After winning this title four times, I still wasn't happy and began to wonder why. I had a good job as auctioneer of the Okeechobee Livestock Market (which is the largest cattle auction in the Southeast). It seemed I had everything going my way but I still wasn't happy. Something was lacking in my life but I didn't know what it was. I do now--I wasn't living in God's will and I believe God has a purpose for our lives and if we live outside His will, we will never be truly happy.

This past year has been the happiest of my life. I have learned so much about God through His word and what it means to be a Christian. He has brought me closer to my family and I know now what it means to walk out of darkness into light. I was blind, but now I see and I praise God for it. Everything I have and every ability I possess is a gift from God. I pray that I can use both to win souls for Christ. Any good that I do, I take no credit for--I give all the glory to God.

Wayne Putnam

In 1974, I came to a place in life that I did not want to go on any more. I was tired of living the way I was, but I didn't know how to change. I had tried being good, but that didn't change anything. It did not make me any happier. I did not know Jesus in any way and I did not want to know Him or anything about Him.

On Friday, November 1, 1974, I went to Dunklin Memorial Camp for the third time in my life. I heard Arthur Blessett share the gospel of Jesus. For the first time, I really heard about Jesus. I fell down on my knees in desperation. I asked Jesus to come into my heart and He came in. He gave me a new way of living.

Jesus didn't change the world around me—He changed me on the inside and gave me peace, joy and happiness. He gave me love for other people that I never had before. But most of all, He is teaching me to have trust and faith in Him, no matter what .

Jim Byrd

To me, Dunklin Memorial Camp means more than the college I went through. I learned how to make a living in college, but at Dunklin I learned to live with the living I make.

There is no doubt about it, life has been more abundant since I accepted Jesus. I accepted Him the day I came to Camp. I believe that's what led me out to Dunklin. I didn't know what was to be offered and I wasn't familiar with the program, but I knew there was a strong force drawing me to be here.

My experience has drawn my family into being a real family. We now have a deeper concern for each family member. This has by no means solved all of our problems, but it gives us a firm foundation to build our marriage on. The marriage classes were also valuable in my life. I enjoy coming back on weekends with my family to the Camp. We have developed life-long friendships at the Camp.

I think that an alumni should visit the Camp as often as possible. It helps the men currently in the rehabilitation program to see that there are those who do make it. A visit by an alumni to the Camp can be an example to others.

The only rest I get is when I come out here on weekends. For anyone who needs rest, and not necessarily from a drinking problem, this is a good place to find it.

"I trust in Your unfailing Love. I will rejoice because you have rescued me. I will sing to the Lord because He has been so good to me." Psalm 13:5,6

Mickey: Another movement we have partnered with is the "Walk to Emmaus". It is a three day spiritual retreat for anyone desiring a closer walk with the Lord. We began hosting the retreats in the early 80's after two friends Harold and Theresa Campbell from Jupiter sponsored Laura Maye and I on a Walk up in Leesburg. We were so impacted by the experience we asked the Campbells to help us get one started for the South Florida area. To date over 100 Emmaus Walk Weekends have taken place at Dunklin. The dining room off of the Good Samaritan building is named in Honor of Harold Campbell who along with Theresa spent countless hours and resources to help birth the local chapter of that worldwide ministry here at Dunklin. The most beautiful thing about Emmaus to me is that the teams who put on each weekend consist of volunteers from many different churches of different denominations and the Lord brings them together every time with such a spirit of unity that it is like a foretaste of Heaven.

In rehabilitation ministry, it is of great value to raise up the staff who work directly with the men, rather than trying to hire them or to use volunteers from the outside.

The need there is for those who have been through the process themselves, and understand exactly what the men are going through. That is not to say that others cannot bring valuable assets to the program, just that both are needed to effectively run a well balanced ministry.   Jesus spent three and a half years training his "staff" and probably most of that time, with only those few men he had chosen as disciples.   t took me a whole lot longer, but by 1985, enough men had gone through the program and stayed on for staff training, that I was able to turn the administration of the Camp over to Hugh Murrow and a full team of trained staff.   Hugh and his wife Christie have faithfully devoted their lives to the Lord working in this ministry for over twenty-five years now. He has carried a heavy burden off my shoulders for many years and cares deeply about the welfare of the men and families at the Camp. Hugh has developed the pallet shop and lumber mill industries into a strong base of support revenue for the Camp.

SECOND GENERATION LEADERS

**John and Sandi Glenn, Ron and Janis Ross, Bobby and
Debbie Huntley, Dave and Gail Garton,
Tony and Marie Bullington, Chuck and Linda Rickards,
Hugh and Christie Murrow, Rich Boggs,
Jack and Garnet Frankenburger**

Now the third and fourth generation of leaders are ready to carry on the Lord's work and we are confident in the men and women who have taken up the torch. I have no doubt that the Lord's plans for Dunklin extend far beyond   after we are gone.

Pastors Terrell and Margie Rowland

Wayne and Tenay Carter

**Braydon, Brenda, Nick and
Kinsey Reynolds**

Chapter 17:
"Striking the Match"

CAMPFIRE

The first Campfire Newsletter was printed in December of 1963. It has endured from the days of manual typewriters to an online presence. In fifty years over 1,500 volumes have been published. It was and is the main source of information about the happenings at Dunklin through the "Camp Blessings" section. Thousands of testimonies of

New Printshop Help (85 years old)
Gift of Okeechobee News

God working miracles in men's lives fill the pages. Articles included cutting edge information about alcohol and drug addiction treatment informed the general population while sermons and Bible studies exhorted believers in their daily walk with Christ. All this was interspersed with a good dose of humor. Up to this year it was assembled "manually" (by men in the program). All the manuals other and curriculum are still printed in the old

Men assembling Campfires

Indiantown bar building, but the current mailing list goes out to over a thousand homes, and is sent off camp for printing and mailing.

WRITING

PHOTOGRAPHING

TYPING

PRINTING

ILLUSTRATING

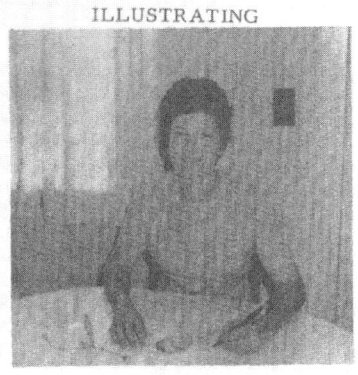

MAILING

CAMPFIRE

Vol. 6   September, 1967   No. 6

THE BLIGHT OF BOOZE

"Who hath woe? Who hath sorrow? Who hath contentions? Who hath babbling? Who hath wounds without cause? Who hath redness of eyes? They that tarry long at the wine; They that go to seek mixed wine. Look not thou upon the wine when it is red, when it giveth it's colour in the cup, when it moveth itself aright. At the last it biteth like a serpent, and stingeth like an adder. Thine eyes shall behold strange women, and thine heart shall utter perverse things. Yea, thou shalt be as he that lieth down in the midst of the sea, or as he that lieth upon the top of a mast. They have stricken me, shall thou say, and I was not sick; they have beaten me, and I felt it not: when shall I awake? I will seek it yet again." Prov. 23: 29-35.

CAMPFIRE

Vol. 5   August, 1966   No. 8

TURN YOUR TROUBLES INTO TREASURES

"And lest I should be exalted above measure through the abundance of the revelations, there was given to me a thorn in the flesh, the messenger of Satan to buffet me, lest I should be exalted above measure.

For this thing I besought the Lord thrice, that it might depart from me.

And He said unto me, My grace is sufficient for thee: for my strength is made perfect in weakness. Most gladly therefore will I rather glory in my infirmities, that the power of Christ may rest upon me. Therefore I take pleasure in infirmities, in reproaches, in necessities, in persecutions, in distresses for Christ's sake: for when I am weak, then am I strong." II Cor. 12:7 - 10.

The Bible says "For the prophecy came not in old time by the will of man: but holy men of God spake as they were moved by the Holy Ghost." II Peter 1: 21 . But I have the conviction that God allowed the writers of the New Testament to experience what they wrote. It was not in air-conditioned studies but along the hot, dusty and sometimes bloody Road of Life that God taught them the message of the Bible.

I also have the conviction that we too must experience the Bible before it means very much to us. We can memorize facts about the Bible without changing our lives but when we experience a revelation of Divine Truth it brings about a transformation in our hearts. In the last two

---

CAMPFIRE

Vol 4   July 1965   No.

BURDEN FOR SOULS

"I say the truth in Christ, I lie not, my conscience also bearing me witness in the Holy Ghost, that I have great heaviness and continual sorrow in my heart. For I could wish that myself were accursed from Christ for my brethren, my kinsman according to the flesh" (Rom.9:1-3)

Modern Christianity knows little and cares less about the burden for souls that weighed so heavily on the apostle Paul's heart. People are more interested today in "tranquilization" than they are "evangelization", and they are more interested in what they can put out of church than what they can put into it.

Men like the apostle Paul, whose heart ached with compassion for lost souls, are rare in the pulpit today. Our master wept as He "looked upon the multitudes as sheep having no shepherd," but few of His "undershepherds" know much about this kind of burden for souls.

I contend, beloved, that Christians will not be of much use to the Lord in Kingdom work until they have experienced a burden for souls. Until we share the burden Paul felt for his people when he

Jail Service: Acts 16:25, "And at midnight:......they prayed, and sang praise unto God, and the prisoners heard them.

CAMPFIRE

Vol 4   April-May, 1965   No. 9

THE PRICE OF REVIVAL

"O Lord, I have heard thy speech, and was afraid: O Lord, revive thy work in the midst of the years, in the midst of the years make it known; in wrath remember mercy." (Hab. 3:2)

In past periods of moral decay and spiritual apostasy the voice of the prophet has been heard in the land, crying out to God for revival. The prophets would call their back-slidden nation to turn from their idols and turn to God in repentance.

When the people heeded the prophet's message to "humble themselves, and pray, and turn from their wicked ways to seek God's face," then God would "hear their prayer, forgive their sins and heal their land," with a heaven-sent spiritual awakening.

The voice of the prophet is again being heard. All over America, God-called, Spirit-filled men, are lifting their voices to warn of God's impending judge-

Logs for the "Country Store," which will be our Refreshment Center for the Friday Night Fellowship Meetings.

ment upon the sins and apostasy of our nation.

God is reviving a remnant of his people who are praying and seeking God's face for a real outpouring of

---

CAMPFIRE

Volume 1   February, 1964   No.

REVIVAL IN A GRAVEYARD

One of the most interesting studies that I have ever made of the scriptures was to turn through the pages of God's blessed Book and read the great Revivals of the Bible... the times when God would more song His people in a spiritual awakening to revive, refresh old regenerate.

In I. Kings 18 revival came when the prophet Elijah climbed Mt. Carmel and re-built God's altar and the Lord sent fire from Heaven. In Acts 2 revival came to Jerusalem when 120 faithful Christians tarried 10 days in prayer. Again God sent fire from Heaven and 3000 people were converted in a single day.

All through the Bible we find blessed illustrations of spiritual awakenings among God's people. These revivals have taken place under varied and strange circumstances, but the strangest of them all, and perhaps the one that most nearly fits our circumstances is the

revival in a graveyard in Ezekiel 37.

2500 hundred years ago the Lord gave the prophet Ezekiel a vision of a valley full of dry bones. The vision represented the "whole house of Israel". Because of their backsliding the Lord had allowed them to go into captivity in Babylon. But God, through Ezekiel's vision, promised to revive and restore his people to the promised land. This, though this vision had its fulfillment in the restoration of the Jews from the Babylonian captivity, I believe there is much we can learn about revival from it. This strange phenomena wherein we can see the conditions for spiritual awakening in any generation.

We have a lot of "Dry bones" in our modern churches today. We have some "funny bones" that are always getting their feelings hurt. We also find some "jaw bones" who seem gifted to rob, back-bite and criticize.

---

1 Cor. 11:31

CAMPFIRE

APRIL, 1974

Liabilities	Assets
Self-justification	Self-forgetfulness
Self-importance	Humility
Self-condemnation	Modesty
Dishonesty	Self-valuation
Impatience	Honesty
Hate	Patience
Resentment	Love
False pride	Forgiveness
Envy	Simplicity
Jealousy	Trust
Laziness	Generosity
Procrastination	Activity
Insincerity	Promptness
Negative thinking	Straightforwardness
Vulgar, immoral	Positive thinking
trashy thinking	High-minded, spiritual
Criticizing	CLEAN thinking
	Look for the GOOD

FOR IF WE WOULD JUDGE OURSELVES, WE SHOULD NOT BE JUDGED

Chapter 18:

Progression of the Program

THE PROGRAM IN 1964

"We plan to follow the basic eight-week program used by most Christian Rehabilitation Camps in the south. We will take men without charge for a period of two months and give them medical and spiritual help.

Three doctors from the Okeechobee Clinic have volunteered their services in treating our men: Dr. Raulerson, Dr. Horton and Dr. Bleech. We will not be equipped to take men who have extreme medical problems, but we will provide basic medical care for those going through the sobering period.

Men who are physically able, will be expected to work at various projects on the farm and camp program. We believe that men help themselves by helping others and each person who comes to the Camp has the opportunity to help build it bigger and better for those who follow. Each man who leaves our Camp, spiritually rehabilitated becomes an encouragement to others who face the same problems.

THE PROGRAM in 1969

Our Camp is open to anyone desiring help in overcoming his alcohol problem. We ask a man to come of his own accord, seeking spiritual help and to stay for at least six weeks in order that he might be built up physically and spiritually.

The object of our work is the transformation of lives through the supernatural power of the Lord Jesus Christ. (II Cor. 5:17). We feel that if a man's heart gets right with God, Christ will deliver him from the craving for alcohol. Medical Science offers plans and programs for the alcoholic, but God offers a Savior.

The daily routine is a half-hour of silent devotion, two hours of Bible study, afternoon work in the Camp's slaughterhouse, laundry, mechanical shop, nursery, print shop, fields or groves and an evening of reading for the next day's classes. There is never any alcohol but smoking is permitted. There is radio but no television. No girlie magazines and no phone calls except in case of an emergency.

We believe they *that wait upon the Lord shall renew their strength.* This is no temporary tranquilizer; it is God's prescription to cure our spiritual confusion. The development of a quiet-time with God every morning can be one of the most meaningful disciplines in our Christian experience. If we are willing to carve thirty minutes a day out of our busy schedule and commit them to God, we can build a foundation under our lives. When we begin each day with a quiet-time with our Lord we can end each day with the confidence that He has walked with us through that day.

To help men in the program cultivate this important habit, we reserve a thirty-minute period between breakfast and our morning Bible study. We suggest they select a quiet, secluded place where they can be alone with God.   Jesus often withdrew from the crowds to refresh himself alone with the Heavenly Father.

It's important to observe the same time each day. Those who try to use their spare time for God seldom develop the discipline for continued devotions. Communion with Christ in the early morning will give you sensitivity to His presence throughout the day.

Read your Bible. We furnish two Bibles to every man who comes into our Camp - the familiar King James Version and also a Living Bible which is a modern translation in easy to read language.

Finally we furnish a New Life Notebook to record the results of his meditation. We encourage each man to write down the impressions the Holy Spirit gives him during his two-way prayer conversations.   Prayer requests are written down and dated and a place is left to record when definite answers have been received. Many men learn to treasure their spiritual diary, and they continue this exercise after they leave the program.

THE RECOVERY PROGRAM *at present*

Presently, The Dunklin recovery program offers long-term, residential treatment for substance abuse with a minimum stay of ten months.

<u>INDUCTION</u>
 Building healthy relationships is one of the main areas of focus at Dunklin, and in the Induction class we begin teaching these skills.

One of the most important aspects of the program is teaching the man to hear from God for himself. Each morning the men are provided with a quiet time in which they are expected to take a soul searching daily moral inventory designed to identify and correct negative attitudes. Contemplative prayer and journaling are introduced by a personal mentor who works with the new student until he masters the skills of listening to God.

Another important element of the over-all program is work. After classes, the men work together on crews around the Camp. Each man's individual task is important to the functioning of the community as a whole. This helps develop a good work ethic. Since work is very much a part of daily life, it is important to learn to work with a good attitude and to take responsibility for those tasks which are assigned.

ORIENTATION

Webster defines Orientation as a turn to the east, and this definition could be a starting point for understanding the Orientation phase of our Regeneration program. A turn towards the east would point you in the direction of the rising sun. A turn towards the "Son" is exactly the goal of the staff of the Orientation class. Through a variety of personal exercises and study each man is guided into an understanding of what it means to have a personal relationship with the Lord.

During Orientation each man participates in the Sociogram where he will learn to give and receive correction. The Sociogram provides an opportunity for men to speak the truth in love, while confronting each other for negative attitudes and behaviors, but also affirm each other's positive improvements

When a man arrives at the Camp he comes from years of being in addiction. At the age a man begins his addiction, is the age at which he stops the normal process of maturing into a responsible adult. To manage his lifestyle, he has often developed entrenched methods of manipulating people.

The Regeneration contract is an exercise in which each man establishes short term goals and learns to apply the twelve steps in his relationships by using three dimensional thinking.
This process requires a man to review his life from birth to the present, focusing on memorable events and the responses and choices he made during those times.

REGENERATION

In this level, men learn the physical and psychological effects of chemical addiction have had on them, and how to take responsibility for their own recovery. They explore the stages of growing dependency on chemicals, and what commitments are necessary on the road to recovery. It includes scientific information on chemical dependency, as well as insights into the damage done to our thinking processes. It is important to understand how the mind has been contaminated in order to understand the controlling effects of addiction.

Each student learns to identify his personal style of building up to drink or drug, and he develops safeguards to keep from relapsing into his addiction.

A man in Regeneration must begin to recognize and learn how to deal with his defense mechanisms of denial, rationalization and projection. Making amends to the people he has hurt and alienated is another part of the Regeneration process.

INNER HEALING

In this phase men learn how to handle deep emotional wounds without medicating the pain with drugs. They learn that the key to inner healing is the application of the Gospel in their lives. Forgiveness is essential to mental health, and the cross is the focal point of all forgiveness.

Inner healing is a prayer therapy which allows God to give us insight and healing concerning certain problem areas of our lives that are related to past events. It does not change our history, but it allows healing to take place in memories of childhood abuse, rejection and fears.

DISCIPLESHIP

The men are in Discipleship for ten weeks, which is the last class in the ten-month regeneration program. Here the men are held to the highest standard. They are the leaders in the program and are expected to live as such. The disciples are given numerous leadership opportunities which encourage a sense of worth. Some of those positions assigned are as dorm monitors, jobsite leaders, and being a big brother to new men coming into the program. They learn that commitment means relinquishing control of their lives to God and how to identify and develop spiritual gifts. They study the stewardship principles of the Christian life.

The married men in Discipleship also receive marriage counseling along with their wives on weekends, while families of the single men have classes to help them understand the aspects of chemical addiction, in order to work toward family reconciliation.

The Single Men's Class is for single and divorced men in the Discipleship phase of the program. It meets two hours a week to teach them how to conduct themselves in a Godly manner with females before marriage and how Godly husbands function in a marriage.

General Education Diploma (GED) classes are also available for men who wish to complete their high school education. After Discipleship the men have completed the program. They go on to graduate.

After successful completion of the regeneration program, further training is available.

STAGE II

The ten-week Stage II program is for those who have graduated the regeneration program, and want the support structure for continuing their Christian growth while deciding the next step in God's plan for their lives. The growth process is evaluated in three areas: classroom, work ethic and living and social time.

Men in this group share their written insights and journaling which brings forth their heart condition and attitudes. This is what God uses to challenge their commitment as able bodied ministers of the Gospel of Jesus Christ.

A man in Stage II is given greater responsibilities on the work site which gives him the opportunity to set a good example for his younger brothers in the main program. They are tested on what they are being taught in the classroom allowing the information to be changed into practical knowledge.

During his time in Stage II each man will have grown in his identity as a son of God with a sense of purpose and vision for his life.

SERVANT LEADERSHIP TRAINING

SLT is for graduates of the regeneration program who desire further training in the field of recovery ministries. To be accepted into the SLT program the graduate must have a clear call by God and the maturity to take on leadership responsibilities.

To be considered for the SLT program, a candidate must first have completed the Stage II program. If accepted into the SLT he begins a journey that will equip him to be a minister in a City of Refuge.

It is a hands-on training program which takes approximately ten months to complete. The trainee is assigned a work site to assist a staff member in supervising a crew. There he learns how to run a crew, minister to men while on the job and exemplify work ethics to younger men in the program. He is expected to deal with his own issues, react appropriately while at the same time minister to the needs of the men in the program. He also has an opportunity to intern in different classes of the recovery program. He is assigned a staff teacher who mentors him in teaching the curriculum while simultaneously ministering to the men in a classroom atmosphere. He, along with the staff teacher, follow up with the men in their dorms, sharing and praying with them. During this time he is given the opportunity to observe the intake interview, learning skills of determining whether or not a man being interviewed is ready to enter the program. This provides a man the opportunity to view the overall operations of the Camp.

FAMILY RECOVERY

The family recovery process is a ten week class set up for the men in the program and their wives. It is designed to help couples detach from attacking each other and hear from the Lord on an individual basis concerning areas of their lives that need healing. Weekend stays at Dunklin's motel soon become a weekly retreat for the families in recovery. Children meet other children who have experienced the same situation at home and build their own network of support among their peers. Dunklin's population swells to over a hundred on the weekends when the families arrive. The dining hall staff provides all the meals and also puts together grocery boxes to go home for those struggling with keeping food on the table. The staff lives on the property so they are never far away if anyone needs them.

Saturday afternoons are set aside as family time, so the men can picnic and play with their children and parents can visit with their sons. We are able to witness the beauty of seeing men playing sports, horse-back riding and fishing with their kids or sitting around a campfire enjoying an old-fashioned Gospel sing.

Each couple participates in Sunday morning classes and afternoon small groups. During small groups each couple finds a safe place in a controlled environment to express their feelings and receive ministry from the team of teachers who serve in the classes. Every staff couple has personally experienced the pain of addiction, and the joy of full reconciliation of their relationship. Seeing these teachers walking their recovery out in front of them brings great hope that they, the men in the program and their wives, too may be healed.

MARRIAGE ENRICHMENT

Upon completion of the Family Recovery classes couples move into the next phase of the process, Marriage Enrichment class. This is where they begin the process of building a strong God-centered marriage. It's as though they enter the class with an empty tool box, and the purpose of the class is to fill their "tool box" with the tools required for getting the marriage building job done. Strong foundations are laid by discovering what spiritual intimacy in marriage is all about. The two individuals begin opening themselves to each other through sharing their spiritual ups and downs, praying together conversationally and listening as a couple for God's specific directions for them.

More tools are added to their "box" as they begin sharing feelings with one another, learn how to handle anger and fight fairly and learn to recognize the needs of one another. Acceptance, affirmation, and many other skills are learned. As each topic is presented the couple then goes off by themselves to make personal application of the topic through an exercise which zeroes in on their marriage relationship. Week by week new tools are acquired. Week by week God equips and trains the husband and the wife to participate in marriage a new way … His way.

WOMEN'S INNER HEALING

The companion class to Advanced Marriage is the Women's Inner Healing Group. Negative past experiences can leave painful imprints on our lives, and the wounds these imprints leave can hinder our relationships. Inner Healing Class helps wives gain a better understanding of how these experiences have affected their marriage and family.

FAMILY DEVELOPMENT

The effects of addiction on the family can at times be too great to overcome during the ten month Regeneration program. Many times the couple has spent their entire married life dealing with the struggles that come with addiction and have not experienced any sense of stability in their home life. Learning to live as a Christian family with a mentor family leading the way strengthens the possibility of long term success.

THE PARENT'S CLASS

The effects of addiction can be devastating on a parent child relationship. Parents often spend many years and thousands of dollars attempting to help their addicted child. Entering the program, the man learns the difference between being a child and a man. A child does what he wants to do, while a man does what he needs to do. As a man, the addict is forced to take a look at the devastating effects his choices have had on his family.

Parents who desire to have a healthy relationship with their son, must also take a look at their part in the cycle of addiction. Unfortunately, many parents have played the role of co-dependent to the addict, enabling him to continue in his addiction and escape the consequences of his choices.   Learning to identify these co-dependent tendencies and seeking to change these behavior patterns is the beginning to restoring the relationship. The Parent's Class is a safe place to find support and guidance from other parents in the same situation.

Parents, no longer carrying the burden of feeling responsible for the addict's behavior, can begin to experience a new relationship with their son. The new relationship is no longer that of a  parent to a child but a parent to an adult son.

Chapter 19:

Creative Contemplations

Swans on Prayer Island built by man in program in 1965

There's a difference here at Dunklin,
I can feel it all around
I'm certain when I come here,
I stand on Holy Ground.
Tools are freely given
And how I choose to use them
Can change my way of livin'!
Sometimes I've been told things
That are pretty hard to take
Learning things about myself
The coldness starts to break
Now that's when things get scary
'Cause I glimpse a better way
But the old me is afraid
To risk it day by day
I've felt rejected, bruised and frightened
By the world of push and shove
But everything at Dunklin
Is measured up with love.
That's the Dunklin Difference
I can feel it all around
The Love that gives me healing
 Has made this Holy Ground.

By Karen F. Pierson

The Last Port of Call

By Joseph Baldwin Haston

They are tired, they are old, and getting no younger,
they are sick, they are cold, and weakened by hunger.
They are wrecked, tossed by dissension and strife,
they are drifting and lost in the backwash of life.
They are deaf and dumb, having given up hope
they have very near come to the end of their rope.
All their strength has been sapped by the life they led,
now their spirits are trapped, they are just about dead.
In this woeful condition they stumble and crawl,
through the door of the Camp,
as close to death they draw.
Here they receive a reprieve from the grave,
if they simply believe in God's power to save.
For they are welcomed in the name of God's Son,
never mind where they have been or what they've done.
A new life has begun
and when they call on His name,
God is faithful and just.
All their past with its shame,
disappears in the dust!
Faith and hope reappear,
where darkness was once before.
Thank the Lord they came here
and found an open door.

I praise Thee Lord that in this world
of malice, hate and sin,
Among thy fold are those who hold
a love for fellow men.
I'm thankful Lord, among Thy sheep
are found a numbered few who care
and in compassion weep
for those lost from You.
But it is sad that there are those
who do not seem to care
when someone falls and loudly calls
for help in his despair.
It seems so wrong among the throng,
are those who pause and grin
to see the fallen in the ditch,
and push them deeper in!
But great is he with humble heart
and void of sinful pride,
who dares the Golden Rule of Life
and brotherhood abide.
Yes, great is he who hurts
to see the fallen lie alone;
who can't refuse to tend his bruise
and shield the pelting stones.
For theirs shall be a recompense
in Heaven of God's rewarding grace,
and here on earth a life
in Jesus' sweet embrace.
I lift my voice to oft' rejoice
that someone came to lend
a helping hand, not a reprimand
and cared to be my friend.
When I too strayed and tearfully prayed
for deliverance from scorn.
C.L. Dane Jones

"HOW TO BE A GOOD ALCOHOLIC
IN 12 EASY TO FOLLOW STEPS"

1. I decided I could handle alcohol, if other people would just quit running my life.
2. I firmly believe that there is no greater power than myself, and anyone who says otherwise is insane.
3. I made a decision to remove my will and my life from God, who didn't understand me anyhow.
4. I made a searching and thorough moral inventory of everyone I knew, so they couldn't fool me and take advantage of my good nature.
5. I sought these people out and made them admit to me, the exact nature of their wrongs.
6. I became willing to help these people get rid of these defects of character.
7. I was humble enough to ask these people to remove their shortcomings.
8. I kept a list of all the people who had harmed me, and waited patiently for a chance to get even with them all.
9. I got even with these people whenever possible, except when to do so would get me into trouble too.
10. I continued to take everyone's inventory, and when they were wrong, which was most of the time, promptly made them admit it.
11. I Sought through concentration of my will- power to get God to see that my ideas were best
12. I believed He ought to give me the power to carry them out.

Having maintained my drunkenness for 25 years with these steps, I can thoroughly recommend them to other alcoholics who don't want to lose their hard-earned status, but wish to be left alone to practice intemperance in everything they do for the rest of their days.

THE FINISHED PRODUCT
OF THE BREWERS ART

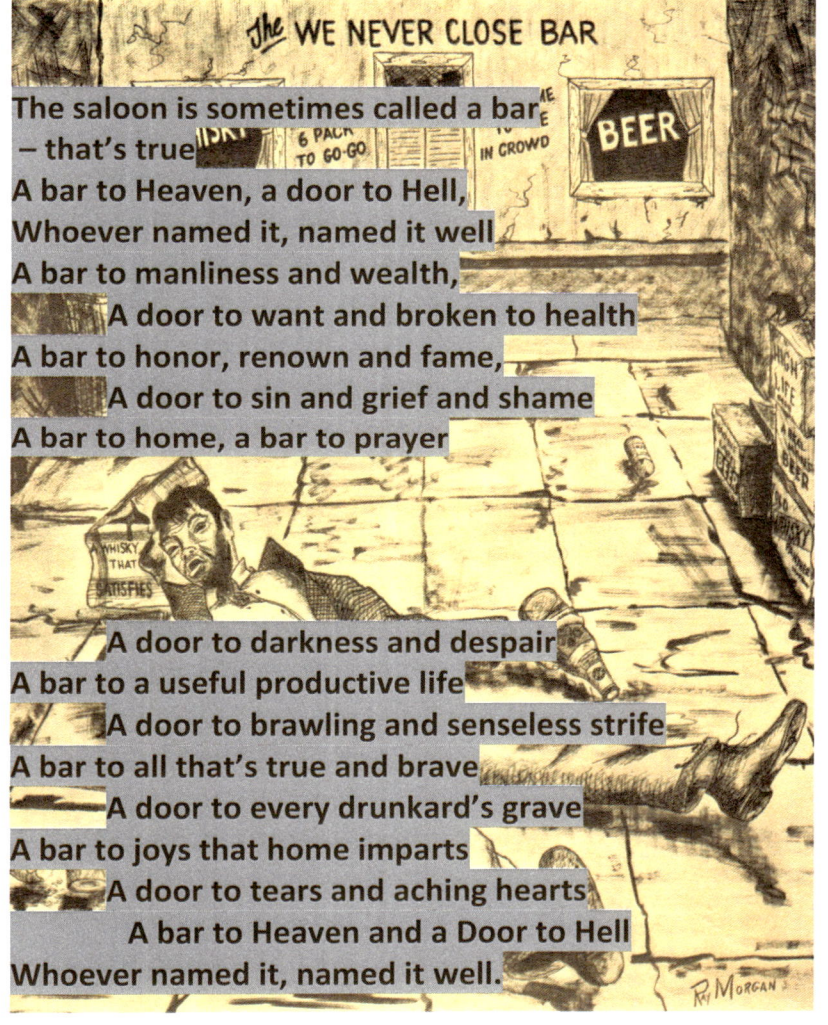

WE NEVER CLOSE BAR

The saloon is sometimes called a bar
– that's true
A bar to Heaven, a door to Hell,
Whoever named it, named it well
A bar to manliness and wealth,
   A door to want and broken to health
A bar to honor, renown and fame,
   A door to sin and grief and shame
A bar to home, a bar to prayer

   A door to darkness and despair
A bar to a useful productive life
   A door to brawling and senseless strife
A bar to all that's true and brave
   A door to every drunkard's grave
A bar to joys that home imparts
   A door to tears and aching hearts
   A bar to Heaven and a Door to Hell
Whoever named it, named it well.

Written by an inmate in the Joilet, Illinois Penitentiary,
serving a life sentence.

The Touch of the Masters Hand

'Twas battered and scarred, and the auctioneer
thought it scarcely worth his while,
 to waste much time on the old violin,
but held it up with a smile;
"What am I bidden, good folks," he cried,
"Who'll start the bidding for me?"
"A dollar, a dollar"; then two!" "Only two?
Two dollars, and who'll make it three?
Three dollars, once; three, dollars twice; going for three.." But no,
from the room, far back, a gray-haired man
came forward and picked up the bow;
Then, wiping the dust from the old violin,
and tightening the loose strings, he played a melody
pure and sweet as caroling angel sings.
The music ceased, and the auctioneer,
with a voice that was quiet and low,
said; "What am I bid for the old violin?"
And he held it up with the bow.
A thousand dollars, and who'll make it two?
Two thousand! And who'll make it three?
Three thousand, once, three thousand, twice,
 and going and gone," said he.
The people cheered, but some of them cried,
"We do not quite understand what changed its worth."
Swift came the reply:
 "The touch of the master's hand."
Many a man with life out of tune,
 battered and scarred with sin;
Is auctioned cheap to the thoughtless crowd,
 much like the old violin,
A "mess of pottage," a glass of wine; a game –
and he travels on.
"He is going" once, and "going twice,
He's going and almost gone." But the Master
comes, and the foolish crowd never can quite understand
the worth of a soul
and the change that's wrought
 by the touch of the Master's hand.   By *Myra 'Brooks' Welch*

A few of Al Cross' Favorite Collected Sayings & Poems

The highest reward for a Christians work is not what one gets from it, but what he becomes by it.

If you marry a child of the devil, you'll have to put up with Satan for your father-in-law.

First, the man takes a drink
Then, the drink takes the man.

It's okay to drink like a fish, if you drink what the fish does!

"He will not grow weary of the Cross who is certain of the crown."

The truest end of life
Is to know that life never ends.   – Penn

...And a couple I'm certain he would have loved:

"We gave God a mess, and He gave us a miracle."
                                                -Terrell Rowland

"A bulldog can certainly whip a skunk, but you know sometimes it just ain't worth it.
                                                - Brian Biggers

One evening in October
when I was far from sober,
dragging home with a
load of manly pride,
My poor feet began to stutter,
so I laid down in the gutter
and a pig came up and
parked right by my side.
Then I warbled
"Tis always fair weather
when good fellows get together"
Till I heard a Lady passing by say
'You can tell a man who boozes
by the company that he chooses'
and the pig got up and ran away!

by
Craig S. Marlatt ©

Down in the land of Okeechobee,
there's a man named Mickey Evans.
Well he takes them old drunks off the street,
and shows 'em how to get to Heaven.
He don't care how they wear their hair,
if their short, maimed, crippled or blind
If they want to get right with Jesus Christ,
Ol' Mickey's got the time.
He's got a sweet little lady name Laura Maye,
and you know that she sure can sing.
And when she tickles the keys on that old piano,
man don't them praises ring?
And you can bet one thing it ain't been too easy,
tryin' to keep up with Ole' Mickey.
But in all a them years, she learned
to shift them gears,
and you know they probably got right sticky!
Well hang on Mickey,
you know help is on the way.
You been workin' real hard trying to please the Lord,
and He's been watchin' you every day
You can rest assured
All your prayers are heard
By the Father in Heaven, in the Name of the Son,
according to His Word!

The Alcoholic's Prayer

A man lay sick on a nasty bed,
with a sick stomach and an aching head.
Alcohol had put him there,
yet he was trying to repeat the Lord's prayer.
He thought that God had done forgot,
but in hopes he prayed to be forsaken not.
Sick and weak he slipped to his knees,
hoping God would hear his pleas.
With a trembling voice he began to pray,
"Oh God please save me before Judgment Day,
oh God, please try to understand,
I want to be with You in the Promise Land.
Oh Lord I know You can save,
in the twinkling of an eye.
And I want to be with You,
in the sweet by and by.
And when that day comes that You judge all men,
I want to be standing on your right hand."
I was saved this morning while in prayer.
And this alcoholic found that God does care.

By Wandle Winderly

273

If Beer Is Such a Temperance Drink...

The many claims for beer, I think
Might need no explanation
If surgeons guzzled it
before a major operation.
If beer is just as advertized,
I earnestly would crave
To know why barbers don't indulge
Before they give a shave
If beer's a drink for learned men
Why doesn't some judge quench
His thirst by having mugs of beer
Convenient at his bench?
If beer's as healthful as I'm told
How strange when he indulges,
A man so frequently acquires
those funny-looking bulges!

Deep within the Swamp lands,
a world is set apart.
A cross upon the wilderness,
a workshop of the heart.
Founded on faith and Christianity
a hallowed ground of Love.
It proudly flies the flag of God,
the cross, it shines above.
Its purpose; rehabilitation –
for men who've lost their lives.
From drink and disappointment
from past and worldly goals.
Its progress ever upward,
its faith a living thing
Its goal : a new born Christian,
Its proof is Christ our King.
Its non-denominational,
Its creed – Goodwill toward men.
Its welcome – Come all ye sinners
let go, let God within.
If you are a weary traveler,
on a sinful road of life,
laden with heavy burdens,
your spirit bound in strife.
The alumni recommend it,
With their testimonial stamp.
Come one, come all,
share in the blessings
of Dunklin Memorial Camp.

A.H. Cogan (1972)

The Left Hand of God

by
Red Coger

When I came to this place,
my spirit was foreboding as the weather.
My life a disgrace, my thoughts scattered
hither and thither
my past, as my garments was tattered and roughshod.
For me nothing in life really mattered,
for I had not felt the left hand of God.
As I stood in the rain, shivering from chill,
I wondered why I had come, if not for God's will.
For upon the ground where I stood,
I knew God's children had trod.
Then a voice to me beckoned me, the Left hand of God
I know it is the left, for as I look back,
all the good people lived on the right side of the track.
There was warmth in their hearts,
no gloom dampened their spirits,
no fears plagued their nights.
But for all of us on the other side of the tracks,
we knew not of God, our future was black
We lived of the world, with sin we did stand,
so that God could not touch us, with His loving right
hand. But hear this lost sinners,
lest our God strike you deaf;
There's hope for all sinners, for God has a left
The alcoholic, the drug addict, the killer, the thief,
Do an about face, kneel down on the sod,
look up to Heaven, and take the left hand of God.
Here in the swamps, on the face of this land,
Is where I call home, where I found His left hand.
Here I found Christianity, compassion and love

Founded by His disciples, on faith from above;
who relentlessly search the Bible pages within
for the right combination, so save the souls of lost men.
Wherever he goes, he's a pilot and preacher,
but to us he has taught, he's our "Brother Mickey".
And as I look back, our chats, prayers and days gone
I might not have made it, if he hadn't urged me on.
Wherever he flies, whatever ground he does trod'
He is an extension of the Left hand of God.

There's a Camp in Okeechobee
Dunklin Memorial is the name;
A "rehab" home for alcoholics,
That puts the rest to shame
No pills or gimmicks needed here
The Word of God is dominant
Of all the books that line the shelves
The Bible is the most prominent
The Camp is spiritual, quiet, serene
It enhances meditation
And Bible study every day
With our Lord the inspiration
I could write on for hours about
The wonderful work that's done
But come on out, see for yourself,
God's praise has just begun!
By Dick Drummond (1972)

Old Scarecrow
AND THE COWS

COWS OF DISTINCTION
CHOISE
OLD
SCARECROW

Let's suppose there were one hundred fifty million milk cows in America. And just suppose there was an industry doing a great business selling a certain kind of hay. This hay, branded "Old Scarecrow", while made from entirely natural locoweed, is alluring described as a sophisticated blend of straw, aged to perfection in the field. As a result, cows by the millions turn from their sober diet of alfalfa and begin chewing on "Old Scarecrow". Now let's suppose that this stuff makes the cows do silly things such as running through barbed wire fences, out in front of cars, and over bridges. So much so – that five hundred thousand are killed or injured each year. Suppose milk production is cut down because the consumers of Old Scarecrow lose fifty million "cow-day" a year from hangovers. Suppose the life expectancy of cows who feed on it regularly is reduced by 12%. Suppose the caring for the cows who have gone loco requires 60% of the farmer's time. And now, just suppose in spite of all this , the merchants of this fatal fodder are allowed to advertise the stuff in every pasture with large billboards displaying "Cows of Distinction" enjoying themselves immensely while chewing on Old Scarecrow hay. And suppose the manufacturers of Old Scarecrow are making an enormous profit off all this trouble and tragedy they cause the farmer. How would you expect the farmer to take all this? Would you expect them to take it sitting down? Or would you expect them to stand up to the producers of Old Scarecrow and declare "That ain't hay!" and then put forth an effort to protect their cows by banning the sale, advertising and promotion of the poisonous plant? And now just suppose we cared as much about our children and fellow man as we would expect the farmer to care about his cows? What do you suppose we would do about alcohol?

By Robert W. Moon

Note: the statistics in this story were accurate for 1967. Today, the picture is even worse. "There are approximately 80,000 deaths attributable to excessive alcohol use each year in the United States. This makes excessive alcohol use the 3r d leading lifestyle-related cause of death for the nation. Excessive alcohol use is responsible for 2.3 million years of potential life lost (YPLL) annually, or an average of about 30 years of potential life lost for each death. * 2012 CDC Fact Sheet Statistics

Bro. Mickey,
Bro. Angelo Masi and
Bro. Ray Zander,

Three Pionneers of the Faith

Dunklin's 50 by Ray Zander

Thank God for the place called Dunklin,
a refuge for those in need through love, sacrifice and prayer
we see this work succeed
Mickey and Laura Maye Evans gave their all to rescue
Those who had no hope and gave up on ever livin'
They suffered hardship we'll never know
By God's Spirit they were drivenMany sought to end their life,
lost family, job and home
With no place to lay their head all they could do was roam
Some tell of being sent to jail
where they felt safe and were fed
They had time to sober up and think of those they hurt,
the girl they loved and wed
They thought of their sons and daughters,
the horrible example they'd been
How his selfish deeds and carelessness led him to deeper sin
While in his cell a Christian put a Bible in his room
He read and felt dirty and guilty, all he could see was doom
He remembered the days he and family
heard God's Word at Sunday School
O how he wished it could happen again
but would God hear the prayer of a fool?
He said "O God I'm but a lost sinner, your mercy I don't
deserve If You'll only today forgive me
it's You I'll love and serve"
This is the story so often heard by hundreds and even more
It's here God gives the victory in this addiction war.
'Prayer Island" is a memorial where many hurting find relief

Where the sinner finds the Savior,
brings joy instead of grief
"Gethsemane Ranch" is where
cowboys learn to ride and
Rope horses and ride bulls while
learning of God's grace
Underprivileged youth are invited
for a week or two
We see a change as God's love they now embrace
The women's "Refuge Ranch" is where
young women turn around
For where sin abounded grace did "Much more abound"
I've heard many stories from those who were once lost
Who found the blood of Jesus paid their fullest cost.
"The wages of sin is death" so each come in condemned
Christ died for them at Calvary, thus their sinful life did end
For those who wish to have a Bible Degree

Dr. Bob can meet your need
It will create a hunger for God's Word
upon which you'll daily feed
You then will be able to teach others
and lead them in God's way
You'll use Scripture instead of logic
which we know will really pay
"Ms. Mary's Home" is always open for
fellowship and prayer
She takes the place of moms or grandmas,
shows all love and care It's like a home
away from home with love, sodas and cookies we've heard
And many are blessed and strengthened
as they sing and share God's Word
For 50 years God's met each need,
we've been kept by His power and grace
His very name is "Faithful" and He'll be that till we see His
faceThis work began with prayer and the answer's so freely
givenWe commend our God to all who hear
for He alone can change your livin'

"Dying to Self"

When you are forgotten or neglected, or purposely set at naught, and you don't sting at and hurt with the insult or oversight, but your heart is happy, being counted worthy to suffer for Christ,
THAT IS DYING TO SELF.

When your good is evil spoken of, when your wishes are crossed, your advice disregarded, your opinions ridiculed, and you refuse to let anger rise in your heart, or even defend yourself, but take it all in patient, loving silence, *THAT IS DYING TO SELF.*

When you lovingly and patiently bear any disorder, any irregularity, any unpunctuality, or annoyance; when you stand face to face with waste, folly, extravagance, spiritual insensitivity and endure it as Jesus did,
THAT IS DYING TO SELF.

When you are content with any food, any offering, any raiment, any climate, any society, any solitude, any interruption by the will of God,
THAT IS DYING TO SELF.

When you no longer care to hear yourself in conversation, or to record your own good works, or itch after commendation, when you can truly love to be unknown, *THAT IS DYING TO SELF.*

When you can see your brother prosper and have his needs met, and can honestly rejoice with him in spirit feeling no envy nor questioning God, while your own needs are far greater and you are in desperate circumstances, *THAT IS DYING TO SELF.*

When you can receive correction and reproof from one of less position than yourself, and can humbly submit inwardly as well as outwardly, finding no rebellion or resentment rising up within your heart, *THAT IS DYING TO SELF!*
ARE YOU DEAD YET?

By Bill Britton

CHURCH AT DUNKLIN

The church that meets at Dunklin gathers at the Tabernacle on Sunday to celebrate what God has been doing throughout the week. It is a place where those who are wearied by the week's labor can come and be refreshed. The celebration service includes praise and worship, corporate and individual prayer, testimonies, the preaching of God's Word, exhortations, program graduations and our famous love (hug) offering time.

During the celebration service, the men in the recovery program and their families, along with alumni families as well as families from the surrounding communities who feel God has planted them here, blend together to form this very unique cross-cultural, multiracial expression of the Body of Christ. As members of this Body come together, each contributing his part, serving as God's hands, mouth, ears and heart, something powerful happens corporately that cannot be duplicated or experienced during one's own personal and private time of worship.

The testimony of John and Kelly Galizewski
that needs no words.

"Welcome Home – Stop in and say Howdy!"

We hope you've enjoyed this book.
Thank you for taking the time to accompany us on this journey.
As you've read these pages it is our sincere hope and prayer
that if you have not been introduced to this "God of Miracles"
personally yet, you will call on Him today. He will meet right
where you are., just as you are .The One who died for your
sins, yet loves you in the midst of them, with a love beyond
anything you could even imagine, is waiting to draw you in to
His everlasting arms.

Lots of Love,
Brother Mickey and daughter Lauralee

PROLOGUE

O' Lord my God,
You have done many miracles for us...
If I tried to recite all Your wonderful deeds,
I would never come to the end of them.
Psalm 40:5

Staff, Board of Directors and Full Time Volunteers Recognition

Ric Aaonosen
Al and Donna Adan
Dr Adair
Jim Anderson
JW and Nancy Adams
Philip Adair
Ric Aaonosen
Sofonias Alvarez
Walker Allen
B.G. and Diane Brown
Allen and Nancy Bryson
Scotty and Kerri Bryson
Chris and Lauralee Bryan
Clifford and Josephine Bennett
Dale and Ida Baugh
David Black
Don and Juanita Burk
Doris Bernardi
Dr. Beech
Fred and Melanie Beeson
Gene and Pat Byron
Gene Byron
Glen Bass
J.S. and Ethyl Barwick
Jasper and Velma Barber
Jonathan Bean
Kim and Thea Bullard
Lester and Theresa Berry
Mark and Beth Burrows

Mike and Theresa Brown * Pastor
Ray and Francis Boggs * Director
Rich and Cheri and Carla Boggs
Robin and Pam Barber
Sharon Bell
Skip and Ginny Bryant
Terry and Shirley Brown
Tony and Marie Bullington *Pastor
Ty Brantley
Ward and Beth Gubler
Walter Karen Cochrane
"Grandpa" Cox
Al and Reba Cross * Director
Allen Carter
Bob and Suzanne Cantwell
Bob and Sylvia Crowe
Caleb and Karen Christian
Dave and Lacey Crooks
Dr. Bill and Mary Cheshire
Ed Conley
Ernest and Stella Campbell
Evans Crary, Jr.
Evans Crary, Sr.
Harold and Theresa Campbell
Jack and Dottie Conant
Jay Cory
Joe and Kelly Cordovano
John and Valerie Canonico
Lil and Lou Carey
Mitch and Eunice Cole
Marty and Carol Carter
Mike Cole
Pablo and Nydia Caez
Ralph and Sybill Crews
T.W. Conley

Vance and Iren Conrad
Walter and Karen Cochrane
Wayne and Doris Cole
Wayne and Tenay Carter
Wayne, Tenay, Morgan, Rachel Carter
Gary and Janis Dickenson
John Diggs
M.D. Durrance
Mike and Mitchell Dobrow
Nick and Erica DeRigo
Scott and Tammy Delaney
Tiny Durrance
Dr. Chip and Mary Edwards
Clint and Nancy Evans
David and Chicky Evans
Dean Evans
Mickey and Laura Maye Evans
Montine English
Doc and Janis Forbes
Bill Frazier
Carrol and Lois Free
Harry Fairbanks
Jack and Garnet Frankenburger
Jeanne Frazier
Mr. & Mrs. Henry Fairbanks
Oliver "RED" Fox
Micheal Fiorella
Robert Gilmore
Staton and Tabitha Grant
Dave and Gail Garton
Hugh and Corene Geiger
Ian and Grace Grove
John and Sandi Glenn *Pastor
Mike and Brenda Grenier
Dwayne and Mary Heaberlin

Al and Karen Hendry
Arnold and Marie Hughes
Bobby and Debbie Huntley
Dr. James Hinton
Paul and Neva Hjort
Fred Helsel
Jim Henderson
Jim Hosea
Larry Henize
Lovel Hitzing
Todd and Emily Haskell
W.A. and Nancy Howell
Dan and Irene Jones
Elsie Janagap
Jerry and Nancy Jolicouer
Karen and Jesse Jones
Lee and Shana Jolicuer
Mallory and Lanelle Johnson
C.J. King
Ed and Joan Khori
Edd and Ernestine Kirkland.
Greg and Sandi Kleinfelter
Monty and Jean King
Steve and Jill Kruske
Dave and Liz Lide
Kevin and Danielle Laughlin
Clarence and Berta Lightsey
David Ladd
Earl Lettilier
Mike and Jodi LaCascio
Rev. George Liner
Rico and Vicki Lamberti
Ronnie and Vivian Laquesta
Wilbur, Mary and Martha Lanier
Richard Lord

Kevin Montford
Larry and Vicki McKenna
Robbie, Toni Hannah Jonah Maddox
Todd and Katrina Mercer
Bill Murrow
Bob and Betty Moody
Chuck and Kathy Miller
Matt and Laurie Moody
Hugh and Christie Murrow * Director
Jim and Elizabeth Mayer
Junior and Betty Mills
Kevin Mumford
Larry and Vicki McKenna
Larry Miller
Tim McGinnis
Mike and CJ McDaniel
Neil & Marcia Meyer
Paul Moore
Robbie and Toni Maddox
Bob and Nell Nettles
Freeman and Shelly Nettles
Ray and Lori Nelson
Thomas and Lillie Nix
Danny Owens
Paul and Nuala O'Higgens
Jeff Prince
Chris and Mary Pugsley
David and Laura Pittman
Don n Peggy Padden
Gene Photos
Jeremy Payne
Terrell and Margie Rowland * pastor
Adrian and Joyce Rodgers
Bernard Robinson
Chuck and Linda Rickards

Chuck and Terri Royal
John and Theresa Roberts
Lawrence and Nancy Rhoden
Loius and Leona Romero
Nick and Brenda Reynolds * Director, Elect
Pat and Purney Raines
Paul Rox
Ron and Janis Ross * Pastor
Terry and Cynthia Reamsnyder
Gordon and Bernice Strongithorm
Guy and Donna Strayhorn
Lane and Leira Strobel
Leonard Smith
Mike Cole
Mr and Mrs Harvey Sampson
Rundle and Cinda Smith
Sam and Phyllis Sehon
Fred and Karen Treadwell
Dale and Deejah Thomas
Fred and Debbie Tuel
Jim and Danielle Tatem
Curt and Linda Taylor
John and Rachel Taylor
Kevin "K.K."Thompson
Patrick and Gail Thwaites
Rick and Kim Trask
Gene and Nell Williams
Andy and Jenna Williams
Frank "Sonny" and Betty Williamson
Hoby and Allissa Womble
Hubert Waldron
Jack and Faye Williamson
Leighton Wilson
Rick Wagner
Roy and Donna Wiley

If I Die Tonight

My Soul Will Be

In H_____ Tomorrow

SIGNED _____

Fill in the place, sign your name, and carry this card with you so that the preacher can tell the truth about you at your funeral.

Note   The Saved Go To Heaven.—*John 5:24*
            The Unsaved Go To Hell.—*Psalm 9:17, Rev. 21:8*

Receive Jesus Christ today—be ready for heaven. *John 1:12*

A tract the men would hand out at an alumni's car station where they would wash cars and share their testimonies.

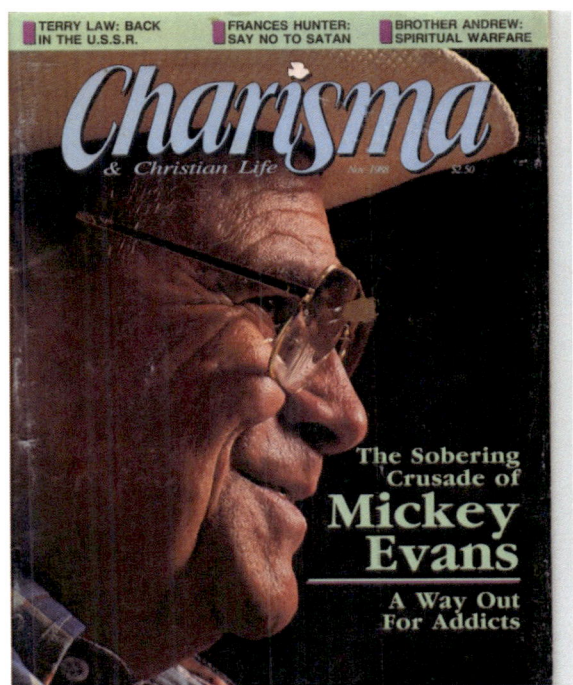

TERRY LAW: BACK IN THE U.S.S.R.

FRANCES HUNTER: SAY NO TO SATAN

BROTHER ANDREW: SPIRITUAL WARFARE

Charisma
& Christian Life

Nov 1988 $2.50

The Sobering
Crusade of
**Mickey
Evans**

A Way Out
For Addicts

world mission journal

PUBLISHED BY THE BROTHERHOOD COMMISSION, SBC   VOLUME 47   NUMBER 11,   NOVEMBER 19

Prayer:
An Answer to Alcoholism

...and the Supporting Strength of Missions

Unique Christian Community

Rising from the Wreckage

By Jim Newton

Surviving Two Plane Crashes: Mickey Evans (left), director of Dunklin Memorial Camp, points out where he crashed for the second time in three months to Reid Hardin, SBC lay renewal leader. Evans said the two plane crashes "were the best things that ever happened to me" and to the camp, because they led to a new sense of community.

In the driving Florida rainstorm, Mickey Evans could not see the power lines as he banked the Cessna 172 to land on the paved farm road at the family ranch near Venus, Fla.

He was the bearer of tragic news. His cousin had been killed in an auto accident. Evans was flying to the remote Florida farm to tell the cousin's elderly grandmother.

In a split second, he saw and tried to duck under the power lines. Too late. The crash was devastating.

As his mother watched in horror, Evans lay on the road with a broken back.

Back in Okeechobee, Fla., at Dunklin Memorial Camp, the reaction was traumatic. Evans had founded the alcoholic rehabilitation center in 1963, and now it was as if the total ministry had come crashing down with the plane.

For almost 12 years, the ministry of Dunklin Memorial Camp located in the heart of the Everglades had revolved around Mickey Evans. Without him, everything seemed to fall apart.

Miraculously, Evans survived the crushed lumber and broken back, and was back at the camp working to rehabilitate the 25 alcoholics there within three months.

"I've learned to live life at a new pace," he added. "One of my biggest problems is that I've been a workaholic since I was a kid."

The painful recovery from the crash has forced him to slow down. "I'm still in pain all day long, and by this afternoon, I'll be having spasms."

But the main thing the crash did was to teach Evans, and all those involved in the ministries at Dunklin Memorial Camp, that they must move toward community, toward sharing responsibilities, rather than depending on the driving force of one man to hold things together.

"We're in a transition period going from rehabilitation to community living," observed Ray Boggs, a burly "dry" alcoholic and construction contractor who serves as administrator at the camp. (See story, page 3.)

Dunklin Memorial Camp — "A City of Refuge where jewels from the Devil's junkpile are polished."

Indeed, Dunklin Memorial Camp is at the very heart of the lay renewal movement in South Florida.

Two closely-related "organizations" have their "headquarters" at Dunklin — Lake Institute and Laymen's Landing.

Lake Institute is not really an organization, but a program, a place, and a fellowship designed to provide deeper spiritual growth and training for Christian laymen of all denominations who have been "turned on" by the renewal movement.

Laymen's Landing, though it is largely non-functional now, for several years was the promotional arm for lay renewal in South Florida. It was composed primarily of Christian laymen who love Christ and who use to fly, and would go anywhere, anytime, to tell others what Christ had done in their lives.

The Christians involved in Laymen's Landing would fly into a town either for a brief testimony before a small group, or for a Layman's Landing Weekend (Lay Renewal Weekend). Southern Baptists involved in the Laymen's Landing ministries now are mostly plugged into the denominationally-oriented Lay Renewal Weekends conducted by the Home Mission Board.

Mickey Leads the Church that Meets at Dunklin

by Dave Van Way
Managing Editor

"I remember driving cattle right through here when I was growing up."

Pastor Mickey Evans, director of Dunklin Memorial Camp in Martin County, reminisced as he drove a dated pickup pulling a long cattle trailer through Okeechobee's downtown recently.

Dunklin Memorial Camp is a regeneration center for men addicted to alcohol and drugs. Evans bought the 300 acres in which the camp is located a quarter century ago. The program has evolved into several ministries, all tied to Dunklin's primary goals.

Evans, a native of Okeechobee, is also pastor of the non-denominational church located in the camp, the newly renovated Old Tabernacle.

Evans says of the church, "It's now the assembly place of a dynamic body of believers called The Church that meets at Dunklin."

Approximately 400 people, most of them men who have completed the regeneration program and their families, meet every Sunday at the church for fellowship, worship and counseling.

The church is the hub

MICKEY EVANS

journals, they meditate on these things, and pray for help in overcoming the negative attitudes which they displayed."

After the quiet time comes classroom instruction, concerning addiction, its effects on the body, spirit and on relationships.

One of them helps feed Dunklin's daily operations.

"We buy them thin and sell them fat," Evans explained as he prodded a fattened steer onto a transport truck.

"We buy quarantine cattle, those which may have been exposed to...

UNDER WATCHFUL EYES: Don Ray, pallet shop foreman, watches a program participant rebuild a pallet.

COWBOYS: A roundup crew prepares cattle for load.

First account of donations

GIFTS VALUED OVER $100.00 DURING YEAR OF 1968

Clark Mattson	CB Radio Sets (New)	$261.00
Earl Turner	Cutting Torch (New)	175.00
Billy Lamb	Saddle (New)	175.00
Louis Reese	pick-up truck (old)	150.00
J. B. Pilgrim	2 head livestock	500.00
Austin Pearce	Angus Bull	500.00
McArthur Dairy	Cows	300.00
First Baptist Church Bartow, Florida	Fogging Machine	300.00
Adrian Rogers	House trailer (old)	100.00
H. Bares	asbestos shingles	$60.00
George Ellis	horses	400.00
David Lundy	Pick-up truck	150.00

Contributors of over $100.00 period Oct. 1-1956-Sept. 30, 1957

Arant, C.F.	$950.00	Ramires, Evelyn	100.00
Bell, Harold	100.00	Reulerson, Arthum	198.80
Bishop, Ethel	100.00	Reese, Louis	110.00
Boney, Henry F.	100.00	Richardson, B.F.	253.76
Brown, B.C.	860.00	Riviera Baptist Church	240.00
Burk, Donald	155.00	Royal, F.B.	115.00
Black, Marion	100.00	Sharpe, J.B.	100.50
Calhoun, David	180.00	Royal's G.Nelsmmh	1000.00
Carlton, Doyle	500.00	Rutherford, Ada	110.00
Christian Church of		South Fla.Timber Co.	108.76
the Brethren	1065.00	Tomlinson, Gilford	250.00
Clewilbs, Steve	115.00		
Conley, T.H., Jr.	150.00	Trinity Temple	148.18
Crosley Houston	380.00	Underhill, Eloise	211.00
Culverhouse, Levita	100.00	Underhill, Mack (T.N.)	380.00
Cumbee, Tom	101.00	Watford, John Ed	100.00
Dickinson, R.M.	355.04	Well, H.N.	293.42
Evans, Donald	412.90	First Bap.Church W.F.S.	119.00
Englishman, Robert.	100.00	Williams, Myrl	156.00
Feilless BaptistChurch	385.28	Williams, R.B.-	800.00
Gay, Eugene	235.50	Wise, Howard	117.70
Godard, Mrs.B.F.	100.00	Williamson, Frank.Jr.	100.00
Ham, Kenneth A.	100.00	Williamson, Jack	108.00
Hamrick, R.E.	264.58	Rock A Bar Construction	149.00
Baleach, L. L.	145.00	Pearce, John F.	115.00
Harris, Ben	100.00	Pearce, Rosa Lee	272.50
Heath, Haywood	199.00	Peete, Henry L.	150.00
Holt, A.T.	380.00		
Kersey, Lucille	110.00		
King, C.J.	1195.00		
Knabe, Mason	155.00		
LaMartin, Robert	105.78		
Leach, Roy	200.00		
Lorida Baptist Church	190.40		
Lightsey, C.T.	2037.67		
McCown, Mrs.J.M.	100.00		
Merrill, Charlotte	100.00		
Miller, Luray B.	100.00		
Miller Memorial Baptist Ch.	106.00		
Montes, Francis	150.00		
Nix, T.H.	255.00		
Northside Baptist Church	174.90		
Olive St. Baptist Church	120.00		
Nelson, Ellen N.	140.00		
Pentland, John	1520.00		
Pine Grove BaptistChurch	200.00		
Price, Louis	216.00		

GIFTS VALUED OVER $100 (NOT MONEY)

Hubert Boros	3500.00
(Building Materials)	
Glen Edwards	500.00
(Dragline)	
Ellen N.Nelson	2600.00
(Hammond Organ with speakers)	

THE CHUMP
(uh. ... Champ)

THE OPPONENT

THE ACTION BEGINS

EASY DOES IT

THE WINNER & STILL CHAMPION

THE END!

For More Information on:
The drug and alcohol regeneration
program at
Dunklin Memorial Camp
Or
Dunklin Memorial Church
(Non-Denominational)

Visit www.dunklin.org

Call: (772) 597-2841
Write: 3342 SW Hosanah Lane
Okeechobee, FL, USA 34974
Note: For GPS purposes :
input "Indiantown" for City

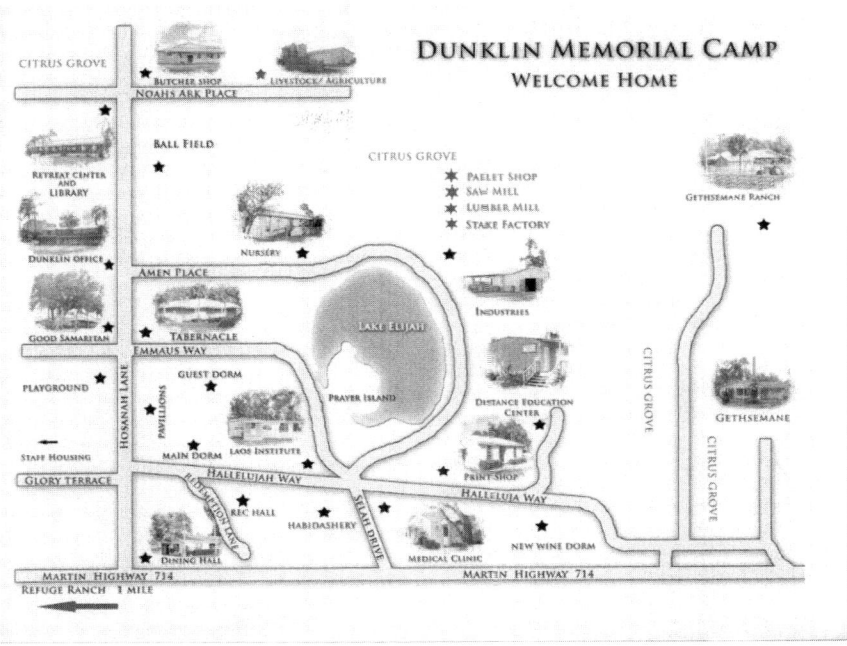

DUNKLIN MEMORIAL CAMP
WELCOME HOME

CITRUS GROVE

BUTCHER SHOP   LIVESTOCK/ AGRICULTURE

NOAHS ARK PLACE

BALL FIELD

CITRUS GROVE

RETREAT CENTER
AND
LIBRARY

GETHSEMANE RANCH

✴ PAELET SHOP
✴ SAW MILL
✴ LUMBER MILL
✴ STAKE FACTORY

DUNKLIN OFFICE

NURSERY

AMEN PLACE

INDUSTRIES

GOOD SAMARITAN

TABERNACLE

LAKE ELIJAH

EMMAUS WAY

PLAYGROUND

GUEST DORM

PRAYER ISLAND

DISTANCE EDUCATION
CENTER

GETHSEMANE

CITRUS GROVE

CITRUS GROVE

PAVILLIONS

HOSANAH LANE

STAFF HOUSING

MAIN DORM   LAOS INSTITUTE

PRINT SHOP

GLORY TERRACE

HALLELUJAH WAY

HALLELUJA WAY

REC HALL

HABIDASHERY

SHIAH DRIVE

NEW WINE DORM

DINING HALL

MEDICAL CLINIC

MARTIN HIGHWAY 714

MARTIN HIGHWAY 714

REFUGE RANCH 1 MILE

If you have any questions, corrections or comments about the book, please email them to:

dmcbook50@yahoo.com

To order more books go to:

www.revmickeyevans.weebly.com

Other Related Links:

www.Dunklin.org

Visit the beautiful Prayer Island at:
http://www.prayerisland.com/

For Gifts go to:
http://www.cafepress.com/+dunklin-memorial-camp

To Connect On Facebook:

"Dunklin Memorial Camp Alumni and Friends"

https://www.facebook.com/groups/91996127108/